Some of my Friends
have Tails

In collaboration with Bill Travers:

ON PLAYING WITH LIONS

VIRGINIA McKENNA

Some of My Friends
Have Tails

♣♣♣

A HELEN AND KURT WOLFF BOOK
HARCOURT, BRACE & WORLD, INC.
New York

First American Edition
Second American Edition

ISBN 0-15-183745-7

Printed in Great Britain

Acknowledgements

♣

The author wishes to thank the Rank Organisation for some of the photographs from *Ring of Bright Water*; British Lion Films Ltd; Jack Couffer; Dare Wright; Ralph Hawkins, Nairobi; Colin Jobson; and her husband Bill Travers for all his photographs, his help and encouragement.

To Bill, Anna, William, Louise,
Justin and Daniel

Contents

♣

Colour Illustrations

♣

Black and White Photographs

♣

CHAPTER ONE

Childhood Years

♣

WE lived for three years of my childhood in a maisonette in Hampstead, with fourteen other animals, including birds and a reptile to be exact. The house was attached to several others of similar character, mellow cream walls and wide steps leading up to the front door, in a quiet residential road of conventional appearance. Did the other houses, I wonder, hold such a strange abundance of life as ours? My own particular territory inside the house, the nursery, held, apart from the usual collection of dolls and other assorted treasures, a large bird-cage in which lived, quite happily as far as one could tell, four blue and green budgerigars. They sang and played and stared at elusive mirror-friends, and were a constant source of delight to me. Now I feel very differently about caged birds—or anything in cages for that matter—and cannot recapture the uncomplicated innocence—or ignorance—of the child.

Cleaning out the bird-cage was not a task I was allowed to do very often, as possibly it was thought my youth meant irresponsibility. Because of this, I was always very careful to do it properly and neatly on the occasions when, heavily supervised. I was allowed to do so. But

S.F.T. 17 B

perhaps the grown-ups were right. One day when I cleaned the cage, and very possibly because until then I had always been so careful and conscientious, my duties were not watched so attentively. The clean water was in the containers and the clean sand on the tray, the fresh food was in the pots, the job was done—and I neglected to close the cage door. The nursery window, too, was open and past my eyes flashed four blue and green streaks, soaring to an ecstatic freedom and certain death. This was my first recorded taste of agony, from which, I believe, sprang my awareness of conscience and guilt.

Below me, on the ground floor, was the territory of my father and the ten other animals. Theirs extended beyond the house through a glass door into the garden at the back—surrounded by a high brick wall and trees. It said a great deal for my father, I think, that all these animals could live so harmoniously in so small a space. Not that it seemed small to me then. It was a world of unending fascination and mystery, and yet one which I accepted unquestioningly. I did not find it strange in the least that living with us in our maisonette in Hampstead should be four dogs, two cats, four budgerigars, a parrot, two bush-babies and a snake called George. It was the world I knew, and was growing up in and, therefore, did not find in the least unusual. The room downstairs was always warm and inviting and rather dark, lined with books and smelling of tobacco and fireside. It was peaceful, yet always filled with movement—dogs going in and out of the garden—cats stretching and rubbing and purring—bush-babies climbing the branches in their cage, and Laura the parrot fussing along her perch, scolding everyone but my father and practising her rather limited vocabulary of words which—perhaps fortunately—I cannot now remember.

The bushbabies were gentle, wide-eyed, nocturnal creatures, the delicate shell-like skin of their ears quivering at any loud noise, filling me with a constant fear that one day the dogs would bark too loudly and the little animals would never hear again. I used to stand and watch them and talk to them, little dreaming that one day I would visit the country of their origin.

During our three years in this house, three of the four dogs remained constant—Tigger, an enormous bullmastiff, and two bull-terriers, Caesar and Coulan. The fourth was originally a Chow, but we did not keep him as I think he became rather difficult, and he was succeeded by a gentle, emotional spaniel called Tasket. The dogs were beautiful and strong; well cared for and well behaved. Tigger was always my favourite I remember—for some reason he made me think of a lion—and so I loved lions even then.

The soft furry shapes of the two cats never involved me to the extent that the other animals did. In my memory they existed as friends one cuddled in front of the fire—one large sandy independent tom cat and one grey and long-haired, of unremembered sex—or stroked as they hovered by your knees in the passage or on the stairs.

Of all these animals my greatest favourite was George. Not that he was particularly communicative, as he spent much of his time curled up asleep in his large glass-sided home. But from time to time we would lift him out and take him into the garden and he would lie blinking into the sun, puzzled perhaps by the air cooling his jewelled skin, or slither slowly along the path in a kind of vague dream. On only one occasion did he become fired with the spirit of adventure and, discovering a small hole in the brick wall leading into the neighbour's garden, he slid towards it with an unimaginable speed and had already half disappeared before I managed to get hold of his tail and pull him back to what we called safety.

I had quite a lot of contact with snakes when I was a small child. Not only because we had one as a member of our household, but because we were regular visitors on Sunday afternoons to the reptile house at the London Zoo. My father knew the head keeper, and we used to go with him to see the snakes, and let ourselves be heavily scarved with snakes of all sizes and colours. They were silken to the touch, warm and very friendly it seemed to me, and I never could understand why evil is represented by a serpent. Of course, the snakes we handled were non-poisonous, and the snake in the Garden of Eden was no doubt of the other variety, but every creature has its weapons of self-defence—or attack if you will. In any event this contact is, no doubt, why I have never had an innate fear of snakes, but obviously do not seek close quarters with those I suspect or know to be dangerous. This attitude I would apply to any species, including humans, unless I had some particular reason for behaving less cautiously!

I do not really know why we left Hampstead and came to live in the country. I don't suppose I was ever told— but one day we left the quiet residential road and arrived in Sussex a mile or so from the village of Slinfold, and only a few miles further from where we live now. Nor do I know why we did not bring George or the bush-babies. I missed them very much.

The country was quite different from anything I had experienced. It wasn't all tidy and neat with grass contained in ordered squares and trees quite regimented and erect, and only a few at that. Here, too, the garden was well kept, and the grass on the whole stayed mainly on the lawn and the flowers in their earthy beds—but the trees in the small wood and at the edge of the lawn were intertwined and tangled, their branches spilling carelessly on to the ground and their colours confused—crowded. Birds were not in cages, but flying free—worms dug riotously without instant reprisal—and the noise of it all! No, not noise—sound. Birds, crickets, wind in the trees—everything was alive, moving, free. Yes, it was the freedom of everything, as opposed to the constraint of everything, which made the greatest impact upon me. Perhaps it was only relative, but then all freedom is relative. No one is really free. We are prisoners of our emotions and at the mercy of the passions that weave themselves into our existence. To be really free one must neither care nor be involved in the destiny of animals and man. I cared very much. And here I too could stretch my wings.

The two years that we lived in Sussex were, for me as a child, very happy. Although I was an only child, I was never a lonely child, and lived a great deal in worlds of my own imagination. The garden and the woods were peopled by characters in the stories I invented; princes and princesses, outlaws and thieves and brave knights crowded under the trees and overflowed into the rose garden and around the pond. I acted all the parts and must have presented a confusing sight to any onlooker— one moment a maiden weeping in distress and next a valiant knight rushing to her rescue. But, of course, apart from an occasional astonished dog, I did not have any onlookers and almost fainted with embarrassment and shyness if my father asked me to recite *Albert and the Lion* to guests. These ordeals made me decide at quite an early age never to make my children, if I had any, perform in any way in front of guests—unless they themselves wished to do so.

One afternoon in 1940 my father called me to him and said he wanted to talk to me. He was very distressed. He sat on a chair by the dining-room window and I sat on the floor between his feet. He told me that the war was becoming very dangerous and that he was going to send me away with my mother to somewhere safe, but that he could not come with us. Nor could the animals. The house was going to be sold. It was my second taste of agony. I looked out of the window and saw my knights and princesses turning pale and melting into the air, and saw the dogs and cats with their trusting eyes vanishing with my father into an unknown future. I did not know how to bear it. Shortly afterwards, my mother and I sailed to South Africa on the *Durban Castle*.

CHAPTER TWO

The Cape of Good Hope

♣

THE Cape of Good Hope was where my mother and I landed in 1940. We brought to it little else but our own hope, my mother's talent as a pianist and composer, and my childish lack of anticipation and pessimism.

In a completely unexpected way, it seemed to me that an even greater and more exciting freedom was awaiting me. The house of some extremely kind friends of my mother, in which we first stayed, was situated halfway up a mountain and gloried in a breathtaking view of the sea. The mountain was my oyster. I could walk un-questioned along my secret paths, among rocks and thick bushy scrub, touching the firm yet velvety flowers of the wild protea. The sun was hot, the earth dry and the bright moist greens of the English garden I knew were replaced by colours of flax and sand and the delicate hues contained within stones. Not only the vegetation, but the insects and animals had changed. Now I saw many coloured lizards scurrying through grasses or pausing in suspended animation on a rock until I had passed by. Chameleons with their independently rotating eyes and subtle camouflage of changing skin tones, patient creatures, ever watchful for the unsuspecting fly or insect. Wise tortoises, isolated from many of the problems of survival by virtue of the home they carried on their backs. The species which I was, I think, most thrilled to see was one which, in another context, I had been most familiar with at home—the snake. When there had been little rain and the ground was parched and cracking as if its lips were opening in a plea for moisture, I had been warned against going too far into the bush and having no shoes on my feet. Of course I never had any intention of going up to a snake and treating it with the same familiarity as I had treated George. I knew that a great many of the snakes were puff-adders and should be left strictly alone. I would afford them the respect that I hoped they would show me. And, indeed, on my walks over the mountain I quite often came across a snake sliding unhurriedly down the stony track or coiled motionless on a sunbaked rock.

These enchanted days had to end and the necessary tasks of childhood had to start once more. School, and because of school, constraint—shoes, pavements, rules and a clock to guide us. It was out of the question for us, in a flat, to have a dog or a cat—why constrain anything else? It was not until I was eleven and my mother could afford to rent a thatched cottage with a marvellous rambling garden and a stream at the side of it, that it was possible to let me have an animal of my own. I was allowed to choose it myself, and I lost my heart to a six-week-old wire-haired terrier, whom I called Blitzy (I kept, in this rather strange manner, the memory of the war with me in my new life). He was a tiny, white, curly-haired bundle with bright brown eyes like polished

Myself with Simon

With Blitzy and Ethel, our cook

The tortoise and his home

Ginny-puppy

Macduff

Macduff and Auntie
Lou

The woods still hold their mysteries . . .

buttons, that looked at you with a mixture of innocence and mischief. Being an only child it was especially wonderful for me to have my own animal, whom I could love immeasurably, and to undertake the responsibilities that come with owning another living creature. Blitzy and I were inseparable and very happy.

He died when he was about two of a very bad attack of eczema. I still remember him very clearly.

When you have loved something very much and for some reason it is no longer there, you don't feel you can ever love or put yourself in a vulnerable position again. But I think that the need to love is an irresistible force and one has to refill the empty place in one's heart. My second dog I chose because he seemed so quiet and retiring and in need of affection. He again was about six weeks old and was a black cocker spaniel, whom I named Simon (I think I named him after Simon Elwes, the artist, who had visited us once and done a pencil drawing of me in a sunhat—I was sitting in the garden getting better after an illness, and I remember he filled me with awe and admiration). Simon—my puppy—was angelic. It was impossible not to love him immeasurably as well. As we ourselves took root in our new home, we began to gather around us other friends. A grey Persian cat which I called Smokey because of her soft grey fur which billowed about her, thick yet fine as gossamer. Belying her demure appearance, she became involved with some rather wild and unsuitable tom cats which lived nearby, and produced two sets of quite unapproachable kittens. We obtained Smokey for no other reason than that we wanted a cat in the house and she needed a home, but

Peter, our Doberman Pinscher, was acquired for a rather more specific reason. I had had a little girl to tea after school and my mother and I drove her home about six o'clock. When we got back we discovered that the house had been burgled. Or rather, an attempt at burglary had been made. All my mother's clothes had been removed from the cupboards and piled into bedspreads on the floor. The burglar must have heard us returning and fled out of the front door as we came through the back. It was all rather alarming and we felt nervous at night for some time. This was when we got Peter. He was a strong two-year-old guard dog with a very fierce bark and, when angry, presented quite a formidable challenge to anyone who approached. He would stand in the middle of the drive, his feet planted firmly on the ground and a ridge of hair on his back bristling skywards. We never had another burglar, and the only new problem to cope with was the fights which Peter occasionally had with the Alsatian next door. Towards us he never showed anything but affection and gentleness. I used to go and sit with him in his kennel after his fights with the Alsatian, armed with cotton wool and disinfectant, water and sympathy, and he would let me clean the wounds, commiserate with him and lie down beside him until he felt better. He and Simon got on very well—perhaps he felt that sweet gentle Simon presented absolutely no challenge whatsoever, and in that I am sure he was right.

Sometimes it is difficult to visualize ever surviving an unhappiness when you are a person who becomes involved with things—people—animals—whatever. Parting from them produces an agony and a desolation from which it is not easy to recover. Sometimes one does not. When the war ended in 1945, and my mother and I returned to England, we had to leave behind Simon and Peter (Smokey had already died a natural death). I can still feel my arms around Simon and someone gently but firmly tearing him away from me, and see the blurred forlorn picture of the two dogs standing beside the house as the car drove away. With my rational mind I knew that we really could not take them back with us. Even if we had decided to endure the six months' quarantine regulations, we did not know where we were going to live or what the future, this time in England, held for us. With my emotions I knew that part of me was being destroyed and that I in turn was destroying a trust. Simon knew nothing of quarantine laws and doubtful futures. He only saw me drive away and knew only the present. Both he and Peter were going to good homes, with friends, but Simon did not live very long—not very long at all. I did not have another dog for nine years.

CHAPTER THREE

Interval

♣

THOSE nine years when I had no animals were filled with the same joy and pain experienced by most young girls growing up. On returning from South Africa I went back to the same Sussex school to which I had been before the war. It was run by two ladies of great understanding and intelligence and I was extremely happy there. My greatest wish when I left school at seventeen was to go to Oxford University, where my father had been, but unfortunately I had not studied Latin in the later years of my school life, and Latin was a compulsory subject for the entrance examination at that time. Our financial situation required that I should train for something by which, hopefully, I could eventually earn my living. Although I had enjoyed being in the school plays— mainly rather ambitious and successful productions of Shakespeare acted in the school grounds—I had no burning ambition to become an actress. Perhaps because I did not have any opposition from my parents! Rather the reverse. My mother was, herself, in the entertainment world, and my father had always been very interested in the theatre, in addition to being very proud of his relationship with Fay Compton, of whom he was a cousin. No, I preferred the widely differing worlds of writing and nursing. Neither materialized. Instead, I did auditions for two London drama schools, the Old Vic and the Central School. I failed the first, which surprised me not at all, and passed the second, which surprised me very much.

The two years when I was a student remain in my memory as completely satisfying in every way. The work was stimulating and absorbing and I had to work quite hard as I was taking a London University Course alongside the school curriculum. This course provided one with a background to acting; the history of drama, of costume, poetry and a certain amount of French drama. In between classes, or if we had a free period, we were allowed to listen to rehearsals in the auditorium of the Albert Hall—for in those days the school occupied a number of rooms in that same building. What riches.

I left the Central School after completing two years of a three-year course. A theatrical agent, who had seen me in one of the school productions, had got me work at the Dundee Repertory Theatre during the long summer holidays, and once I had become involved in the live theatre I felt I must stay on—this must now be my school. The theatre was beautifully run by A. R. Whatmore—Whattie—and one could not have found a better teacher. From the maid in *The Heiress* to the innocent heroine of *Northanger Abbey* and on to Estelle in *Great Expectations*, with new plays every fortnight, there was no lack of variety or challenge. It was while playing Estelle in *Great Expectations* that Daphne Rye, the Casting Director of H. M. Tennents, came to Dundee during a tour she was making of some of the repertory theatres. I could not have been more unhappy. For the past fortnight I had been suffering from a series of boils and, at this particular moment, I had a large one distorting one side of my face. Apart from making me look rather grotesque, it was quite painful, and on the night Miss Rye came to the theatre I felt anything but my best! Luckily for me, she wasn't completely deterred, and I was offered the part of Dorcas in John Whiting's new play, *A Penny for A Song*, in London at the Haymarket, with Marie Lohr, George Ralph, Ronald Squires, Denys Blakelock, Ronald Howard and George Rose—a list to intimidate the most courageous! I cried bitterly when I left Dundee. Another doubtful future lay ahead.

From 1950 to 1958 I worked constantly—plays in London, films, television. Some unforgettable and wonderful experiences—Charles Morgan's *The River Line*, with Paul Scofield and Pamela Brown, and the 1955 season at the Old Vic, in which I had the chance to play Rosalind in Robert Helpman's production of *As You Like It*, as well as somewhat less memorable endeavours, chiefly in films, but from which I learned a great deal—mainly to be selective. Work was everything—it was my life—and although I was working for other people and with other people, it was very much a one-dimensional existence. Probably selfish. It is only in loving someone or something that there can be perspective in life. At the end of these nine years I was given a present—something I needed very badly.

CHAPTER FOUR

A Question of Involvement

♣

SHE was always referred to as Ginny's puppy, and for some unknown reason remained Ginny-puppy for the rest of her long life. She was a small, adorable eight-week-old black poodle, who came everywhere with me; to the theatre, on tour, and once I even smuggled her into a cinema, which she found an intensely boring experience, until Marilyn Monroe appeared on the screen.

When she was about two years old we thought it would be a good idea for Ginny-puppy to get married. So we found her a handsome husband and to our delight she soon developed a comfortable matronly figure, while losing none of her youthful characteristics. It was winter and snow carpeted the ground. I was staying in Cornwall with one of the sisters of Bill Travers—whom I was later to marry. Ginny-puppy was, of course, with us, and it was quite apparent that her puppies would soon be born. Why do these things always happen at night? About 10 p.m. she started fussing around the study where she was sleeping, making imaginary nests behind the curtains and generally behaving in a rather distressed manner. There was no question of going to bed oneself, and I gathered together a collection of towels and newspapers and sat down to wait. By about six in the morning three puppies had been born—three smooth-haired black bundles who squeaked blindly around Ginny-puppy as she lay exhausted in her box. Cindy, Lou and Memo. Ginny-puppy found motherhood rather confusing, I think, and never entirely accepted that these three new lives were now her responsibility. We could not keep four dogs in a small flat and so we gave Cindy and Memo away to friends and kept Lou. Lou—or Aunty Lou as she later was called—was a strange little dog, rather narrow and small, and we were advised not to let her have children. She had a great deal of courage and a good sense of fun, and an inexhaustible supply of affection. She and her mother got on very well.

In 1957 my life changed—or perhaps became a fulfilment of childhood longings. Probably in both Bill and myself there had always been a submerged desire to escape from the concrete jungle, the pressures of sophisticated society, the rat race or what you will. Even at the beginning of our life together we found ourselves leaving London at every available opportunity and driving out into the country to sit in a field or dream over a ruined cottage.

Our cottage took us two years to find. We stood in front of it and looked across the fields to where, beyond the blue-grey distant hills, lay the sea. We could see no house, hear no noise. No human noise. Around us was a tangle of azaleas, rhododendrons and brambles, beside us a cool green wood hazy with bluebells and behind us this pale, brown cottage. The sharp, pink sweetness of rambler roses spilling over the faded green door. It seemed to us that all joy, all perfection was crammed into this one corner of the earth—birds were calling, insects and bees humming, reminding one of childhood summers when one lay in the buttercup grasses and looked at the sky through a web of twisting stems.

We have lived here for over twelve years, and apart from the house changing shape and enlarging—as our family did likewise—and the peace of the sky being more frequently disturbed by intrusive aeroplanes, everything is much as it was. We can still see no house, and the blue-bell woods still hold their fragrance and their mysteries.

If you allow it to, the country and what you feel for it can take you over—you can be fulfilled and satisfied without personal ambitions or strivings playing any part in your life at all. It is all a question of involvement and loving, and if you let your involvement and your love grow stronger, your need for nature and natural things will increase, not diminish. As I write this I am sitting in a caravan in the garden, the top half of the door is open and sun and air are pouring through towards me in great sparkling surges. Insects and birds and tardy butter-flies are skimming and hovering outside in their sunny freedom, and the trees are serenely unloading their burdens of gold and yellow leaves, knowing they will return next year in their fresh green coats.

As my love and need has grown with each passing year, so it has become more difficult for me to leave this corner of England. With children of one's own, animals and with personal fulfilment, the need for self-expression in the outside world has grown rapidly smaller. In 1964 it was, perhaps, a little bigger than it is now—not so much the need for self-expression, but the unwillingness to resist challenge.

Hitherto, the animals within my personal world had consisted of dogs, cats, birds and fish. At our home at the time we had two dogs—Ginny-puppy and a male from her second litter named Boy. Boy was a very special dog, shy and humble with new human friends, yet fiercely protective of both us and his territory against all suspected intruders—of whatever species. Our cat was a proud, independent and shining black creature called Macduff, whom we acquired when Bill was at Stratford in 1962 playing the part of that name. A marvellous companion, he would accompany us and our piggy-back children on our long walks through the woods to the mushroom field, where those small white early-morning prizes were to be won. Four goldfish, who blinked peacefully at you from their watery world, completed our family. Aunty Lou was no longer with us. When she was seven years old she had become blind. At first we could not believe it, but within three days she had changed from a joyful active little animal into a trembling lost soul, completely dependent, and for some reason unable to adapt herself. Probably because the change in her life had been so dramatic. She used to stand crying in the middle of the room and one would have to pick her up and carry her about the house as she couldn't bear to be alone. We made no hasty decisions, but after a time it was clear that she was no longer a happy little dog. Deliberately to end an animal's life always arouses controversy, both inward and public, even if it is to end suffering, mental and physical. One can only act with integrity and live with one's decision and with the loss such decision brings.

Now, one foggy March afternoon, we were being asked to go to Africa to work with animals of a very different kind—lions. We could take our children with us, but we could not take our animals. Ginny-puppy was very old and her health was rather delicate, we did not know if we should see her again. It was very difficult to say good-bye. We left them all in the tender care of Bill's father and we sailed for Africa filled with ignorant optimism.

This Africa was quite different from the one I had known as a schoolgirl. This was East Africa—peopled more by animals than humans—still filled with mysteries of nature and of the African himself. A great deal has been written about the making of the film *Born Free*—Bill and I have written briefly about our experiences in a book called *On Playing with Lions*. That book was written in 1966, a year after the film was completed. In retrospect one's evaluation of those past experiences does of necessity alter, emotions and convictions have, on the majority of questions, matured and deepened. At the time we made *Born Free* neither of us had had any occasion to work with animals—unless one counted the spaniel Flush in the film of *The Barretts of Wimpole Street*, who had practically nothing to do with the human cast and was completely under her trainer's command. *Born Free* was to be made in Kenya from Joy Adamson's universally known, best-selling book which told the story of the relationship and life shared by Joy and her game-warden husband, George, with a lioness, Elsa, from the time she was a tiny cub to when she was a mature and magnificent animal with a family of her own. In retrospect we see that *Born Free* was not an end in itself, as we probably thought at the time— we believed then that the incredible experience of working with the lions in the particular way we did, and our close contact with nature, was a crystallization of a myriad of our half-conscious thoughts and feelings and longings. We certainly did believe, without a shadow of doubt, that afterwards our lives could never be the same. We could never be the same. What we did not appreciate was the extent of the impact of this crystallization.

George Adamson, the unique and very human being, whose attitude towards lions, and indeed all living creatures, was our chief influence during those very difficult months of filming, will always be a guiding light to us on questions of animal treatment, animal-human co-existence in the world and many other questions besides. I firmly believe that if he had not been there the film would not have been made—on the basis that it was made. Probably a film of a different type could have been produced, with tricks, split screen and—as indeed was at one point suggested to us—no close contact with the lion once it had grown up. We knew we could not be part of this kind of thinking; we knew that what we felt was the right relationship between us and the lions of friendship, affection, respect was one that George and Joy Adamson had already proved to be possible—with Elsa. We knew, of course, that their experience of this kind of lion-human relationship had been mainly centred in that one animal. But we did not feel deterred by the lack of quantity—quality was the key. The human-animal relationship which we had originally been asked

36

Girl and Ginny on the plains

Joy at Elsa's river

to participate in was based on human domination. When I look at photographs taken of us in those early training days, leather guards round our wrists and sticks in our hands, I realize how dramatic the policy change had been when the decision was made not to use circus lions, but what we used to call the 'Kenya Lions'. Domination can never be a substitute for love, nor fear for trust.

No, *Born Free* was not an end in itself. Elsa was the beginning and *Born Free* was the next link in the ever-lengthening chain of discovery. On the premise that no animal film had ever been made that way, therefore never could be, *Born Free* would have continued in the animal film tradition. But, miraculously, the pattern was changed. Now the next link could be forged.

George Adamson has lived for the past four years in the Meru Game Reserve. He has been helping some lions to become independent of man, to learn to live in freedom within the context of nature's own laws. The three original lions he took with him were three we used in *Born Free*—Boy, Girl and Ugas. These, after a short time, were joined by four cubs, one male and three females, who had been personal pets but whose owner believed in George's work. Girl subsequently mated and produced two beautiful lioness cubs, Maya and Juno, and, more recently still, she had another cub, Sandie. There are now ten lions in the pride. They are wild. They have established their own territory, they supply their own food and fight their own battles. Elsa was not a unique case; George has proved the rehabilitation of lions possible. It could be, perhaps, applied to many other species which are fast disappearing, even from this very beautiful, remote area.

I do not know whether Meru has such appeal for me because it is so attractive or whether my interest is heightened because of the associations the reserve awakens in my mind. This is where the Adamsons lived with Elsa, where she mated, reared her cubs and eventually died. When I had finished filming *Born Free*, Joy Adamson took me up to the reserve for three unforgettable days and involved me in her own personal memories of Elsa and their life together in a way that had not been possible during the intensive months of filming. We walked through the dry snapping bush, vibrating with life, and climbed Elsa's rock where she used to sit and where she eventually had her cubs. A tiny bird was nesting on the bare face of the rock. I was suddenly aware that no part of nature, however barren, is without some use. It must have been very hard, I think, for Joy Adamson to let an actress she had never met interpret herself and a part of her life which had meant so tremendously much to her. I have always been touched by the confidence and trust she placed in me at that time, which culminated in this very personal visit to Meru.

We walked down towards the coolness of the river, pale amber where it sped over the rocks, and darkening in colour and intensity where the rocks fell away and the water caressed unknown depths. As we pushed aside the branches of overhanging trees and trailing creepers which insinuated their way around our shoulders and arms, we surprised a lone crocodile resting on the shore. Belying his long craggy appearance, he moved with the speed of a kestrel swooping on its prey and with barely a ripple he had disappeared into the water. When Joy suggested going for a swim, I didn't immediately enthuse over the suggestion, my mind conjuring up a picture of grinning eyes and eager teeth awaiting my vulnerable feet. However, she assured me that she would choose a pool where nothing else could enter, least of all a crocodile, and we spent a strange and wonderful time lying in the jewelled water, letting its coolness slip over us, hearing the shrill cries of birds and the chatter of baboons— and knowing that this was the river across which Elsa had brought her cubs to the Adamsons for the first time. This, too, was the river near where she died. Her grave is not very far from the river—not many people have seen it—and it is surrounded by a high thorn fence to stop the wild rhino damaging the grave stones. It is a place of great simplicity and beauty and I can never forget it.

The scene of our animals at home was a changing one. While we were in Africa filming *Born Free* our fears were realized and Ginny-puppy died. She had developed an inoperable tumour some time before we went away and our veterinary had told us there was little we could do about it except ease the pain when the end drew near. To arrive home without her laughing little face to greet us was more difficult than any of us cared to admit.

Surrounded as we were in Africa by animals of all descriptions, we felt very lost in our home without a dog. So we answered an advertisement in a local paper which was searching for good homes for Border Collie puppies. We drove one Sunday, our day of rest, to a fascinating farm near Thomson's Falls, owned by the Hon. Violet Carnegie. She bred angora goats, and if you didn't know you were in Kenya you might have been in Wiltshire! She was very charming and asked us to join the family at their picnic by the river, after which we could choose a dog. We would really have liked to take them all—and probably would have if the thoughts of transport to England and subsequent quarantine hadn't added up to a rather expensive operation! There were five puppies—all endearing, all begging you with their bright little eyes to take them—it was an impossible situation. So we let the children decide. They looked carefully at all five of them and to my joy they chose the one that seemed most timid and needful of love. We called her Nell—it seemed to go so well with Nanyuki, the name of the little village near where we lived. Nell of Nanyuki is now very beautiful and self-effacing and rounds up the children with the same calm efficiency as she would have her own herd of sheep. She it was who filled the gap in our home and our hearts left by Ginny-puppy.

CHAPTER FIVE

A Statement

♣

A YEAR and a half after we had returned to England, and after hours of conversation, of which the subject was to a great extent our lions and their fate—those which had gone to zoos and those which had gone to George—Bill had an overwhelming desire to tell the story in a film. Sometimes in life you have to make a personal statement —if you are an actor you can sometimes make it through the parts which you portray—but there comes a moment when this is not enough. The statement must be recognized as being your own, and stand or fall on its own merits. To make a statement on film needs money, and we found that with our savings we would just have enough. A one-hour television special in colour was the aim. Bill was extremely fortunate in having Ken Talbot, who had photographed *Born Free,* as his cameraman. I was unable to accompany Bill on this trip as I was expecting our fourth child early in the following year, and the five weeks he was away was a time, for me, of wild speculation over imagined dangers.

When he returned he had twelve hours of film! Some exciting, some extraordinary, some repetitive—but one thing that showed very clearly, apart from the remarkable character of George Adamson himself, was that Bill's old friends still remembered him. Ugas, Boy and Girl still greeted him, still accepted him after one and a half years. Even the four lions he did not know accepted him; such is the influence of kindness and trust.

George's camp is fairly primitive, but then in the heart of the bush, living with lions and weaver-birds, the so-called comforts and luxuries of life seem superfluous. When I visited the camp in 1968 certain 'modernizations' had been made, but when Bill went out at the end of 1966 one had to walk past the lions—any who happened to be around—armed with a spade and a roll of Bronco and take one's pick of the most secure-looking bush. At night a torch would be added to your equipment. The fence around George's territory was really unworthy of such a name, and the gate had a good six-inch gap between itself and the gatepost, so almost anything could have got in if it had wanted to. In fact, on one or two occasions some of the lions did get in, which was all right if they had been invited, but a bit trying if one was getting un-dressed to go to bed or doing one's teeth.

The film was almost entirely shot 'as it happened'. When one realized that they were working with mature lions capable of doing tremendous damage had they so wished, then one could appreciate the possible hazards of the situation. That there were so few difficulties was due, I am sure, to George's and Bill's philosophy and love of animals.

To offset the African scene, Bill filmed one or two scenes at our home. But to make a violent impact at the beginning of the film we went to Whipsnade Zoo to record an 'as it happened' meeting between myself and Mara and Little Elsa—two of our *Born Free* lions who had been denied freedom. It was two years since they had seen Bill and eighteen months since I had paid them a painful, heartbreaking visit.

It was quite probable that they would not remember us—which would, I suppose, prove something to the people who believe that animals do not have memories. We arrived as the zoo opened, early one cool spring morning. Very few people were around. We walked to the lion compound, taking care not to let the animals see us—and we recognized, without any difficulty, our two old friends. The camera was in position and I walked to the wire calling their names. Somewhere in their minds a chord of recognition must have started to hum— for they lifted their heads and ran towards us as they had some eighteen months before. They moaned and cried and lifted their front feet against the cage—but I could give them no touch of comfort, only call their names and feel again the agony of betrayed trust. The impact was made.

When the work was finished, Bill had the almost insurmountable task of editing 25,000 feet of film. Where on earth did one begin? Fortunately, he was joined at this stage by James Hill, the director of *Born Free* and a personal friend. Together, for many months, they worked on the film, selecting, discarding, changing, worrying—until they had turned twelve hours of confusion into a one-hour television special called *The Lions Are Free*—it was sold (rather appropriately) to British Lion Films, who in turn sold one showing of it to an American network. It was a very important achievement for Bill—it meant he had been right to have had the courage to make his statement and that now he had the financial means to make another if he so wished. But it meant something else as well—it meant that unknown thousands of people became interested in his views on animals, the rightful part they play in the world, the need for mutual trust and dependence, the horror of a world without them.

That these people exist we know now from the hundreds of letters we received after *Born Free*, *On Playing with Lions* and, later, *Ring of Bright Water*. Of course, there are many wonderful societies which devote their entire time to caring for animals, whether wild, captive or pet, but sometimes a truth can only come home to a person if he becomes involved, and one of the most effective ways to achieve this is to tell a story on film.

The work that we did before we started to form the next link in the chain was very interesting, great fun, but for us lacking in the deep fascination and involvement that we now seemed to need. It almost seemed that humans were not enough—or too much if you look at it another way! I cannot quite remember when exactly it was that we found ourselves deciding to leave home once more.

Giraffe at Samburu

CHAPTER SIX

Reflections in the Water

♣

SOME time before we had read a very extraordinary and
sensitive book called *Ring of Bright Water*. We had both been
stirred, not only by the relationship the author, Gavin
Maxwell, had with his otters, but by his deep love of
nature and his awareness of the things which really are
important in life. At least to us, too, they seemed important.

We left our animals and our home in the care of friends
and one Monday evening piled ourselves, our children,
our governess, our luggage, children's bicycles and a
strange assortment of bags and baggage into the sleeper
train from London to Perth in Scotland. Both my grand-
mothers had been Scottish, Scotland was where I had
first started to work—it was a land to which I felt I partly
belonged and which I wholly loved. I felt very happy to
be going back.

The house the film company had rented for us was
eleven miles outside Oban. We had already spent a
glorious three hours driving from Perth to the West
Coast—snow-topped mountains, lochs and forests of
purple and green mystery speeding by our windows. But
nothing prepared us for the moment we drove up the

drive of Muckairn—the home of Mr and Mrs Ronan Nelson and which was to be our home for the next four months.

It was early April, ice blue sky and golden sunshine. The air was fragrant with the scent of the hundreds of daffodils and narcissi which lined the granite stoned drive. The way ran steeply between trees and over a burn —silver, enticing, filling our young fishermen in the family with gleeful anticipation. (They caught quite a few fish but returned them unscathed to their watery world.) As the car climbed slowly up the last curve of the drive, a sight of inconceivable beauty exploded before our eyes. A wide green lawn sloped gently down to a riot of azaleas, rhododendrons and a surging yellow and white sea of spring flowers. Beyond this feast of colour, a loch shimmered into the far distance, reflecting in its mirrored surface the purple hills and trees of the shore, and the gently moving white clouds of the azure sky. Not far out from our side of this entrancing expanse of water was a little low island, on which grey and shining shapes seemed to be moving. We laughed in disbelief. It was too much to take it in all at one time—that this friendly, mellow stone house on our right was to shelter us, this garden filled with marvels—some seen and some still hidden from view—was ours to walk in and explore and that this island, on which the smooth grey seals were now lying, was within our new-found territory. All we had to do was to launch the old green rowing boat, nestling unused in the boathouse by the lochside, and, armed with tins in case we shipped any water in our enthusiasm to get a closer look at these appealing new friends, row as quietly as possible out towards them. The first time we did this the seals seemed a little shy and slid into the water when we were still some distance away. But someone told us that seals love singing, and after that useful information each trip brought us closer, the air ringing with our eager but breathless voices as we pulled at the oars and sang 'Over the Sea to Skye'. After we had been there only a few weeks, the seals would let us approach almost to the island and only at the last moment would they disappear into the dark loch, bobbing up near the boat to look at us with their kind eyes.

While the rest of the family settled into the house and explored the secrets of the garden and the shore, Bill and I began to make acquaintance with our new working companions. The six otters which were comfortably installed with their owners, Mabel and Tom Beecham, and their son Gary, in a house and garden not more than two miles from where we were staying, had all been brought from America. They had been reared by the Beechams, to whom they were devoted, and all possessed strong individual personalities. There was one other otter, called Oliver, who had also come from America and was in the charge of Hubert Wells who was the trainer for Jonnie, the springer spaniel. Jonnie was to be my dog in the film.

The methods that we had used for getting to know lions we applied almost without exception to getting to know otters. Otters are not lions we were told on more than one occasion—which we were well aware of—but we found little difference was needed in our fundamental attitude towards them. Time and trust—these were the basic requirements. If you were lucky, and you had enough time, enough contact, you might even have affection—but trust, I think, was still more important. When you meet an animal who has not previously, or recently, had a close relationship with another human being, the chances of affection developing are quite strong. These otters, as I have said, were personal pets of the Beechams, and therefore it was unlikely one could progress much further beyond trust and acceptance. With the dog Jonnie it was different. He was two years old and had lived in kennels all his life. He was one of many other dogs sharing their owner's time and affection and he had never been deeply involved with a single human being before.

Each day we used to go up to visit the otters, concentrating on one beautiful female named Dusky ('Dusky' Springfield as Bill used to call her) who was the most easily handled and most likely to respond. We sat around in the compound, which enclosed a very large area of grass, shrub, trees and a stream, well wrapped up against the keen spring wind, making no obvious overtures to her, but showing pleasure if she approached us, which she did from time to time, emitting a series of little questioning grunts, or pausing to sniff a shoe or a trousered leg. Sometimes we took a toy with us—an old piece of sacking, a plastic bottle, a ball—anything to divert, to amuse, to make the time she spent with us happy. Otters are rarely still—the moments of quietness one can spend with a dog or a cat, or even a lion, are seldom experienced with otters, unless one knows them very well indeed. On this occasion we did not have time

A beautiful female called Dusky

Bill managed to
establish a real
friendship

Jonnie had a lot of affection

Nell

Releasing the cygnet

Off to work

Louise and Bambi

Jonnie was an excellent mother

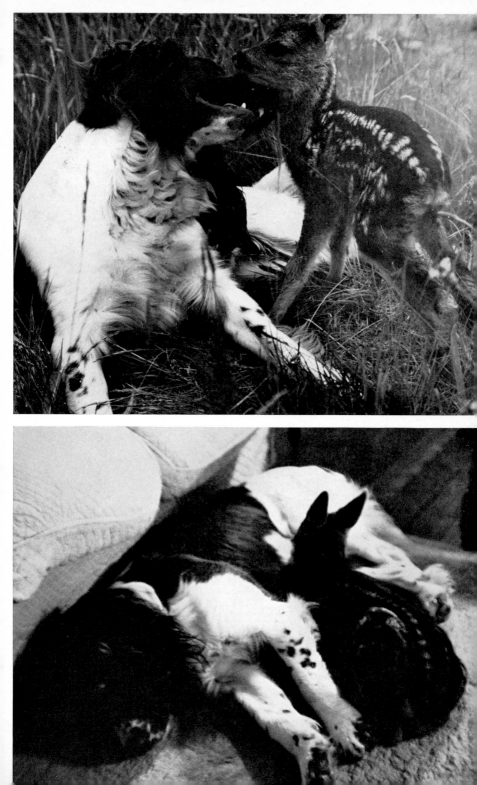

Jonnie and Dusky and their director . . .
Jack Couffer

to get to know them that well, although Bill managed to establish a very real friendship with Dusky. He always had a great deal of patience and they knew they could trust him. I did not have to know the otters to the extent that Bill did, but I did have to have a very close relationship with the dog.

When we first visited the otters, we used to see Jonnie in his kennel and go and talk to him and take him out for a walk—but I knew this approach would mean little in terms of creating any bond between us. So I asked permission to take Jonnie back to Muckairn to live with us. The following day, after our walk with him, he came back to our house, and to a new life. During the day there were no problems—I worked hard to establish a firm relationship, one that would work and that would be fun as well. We walked together along the edge of the loch—Jonnie running free, investigating the new and intriguing scents with a damp quivering nose, his whole body vibrating with energy. Then I would call him to heel and insist that for a time he must walk beside me. He was a willing student and learned his lessons quickly. He would sit still on the path while I walked some distance ahead, and would not follow me until I called him. Then a tangled whirl of brown and white would fly along the path and we would indulge in a delighted greeting—as if the separation had been for weeks and months instead of seconds. Jonnie had a lot of affection to give. He became my shadow. He was required to go in a rowing boat in the film, so we used to go out on the loch in the old green boat—I often wondered who was more amazed by this new proximity, Jonnie or the seals!

He used to watch them, head on one side, as we rowed past the little island on towards another steeper rocky outcrop where the gulls and the terns cried and called and nested. The echoing air cut sharply by the flight of the more nervous rock dwellers, disturbed by the dipping splash of my inexperienced oars.

Full days—and broken nights. Jonnie did not take at all kindly to being parted from us and left in the warm kitchen for the night. Perhaps he thought each night brought an end to his new friendships and the passages rang with his desolate howls, bringing us out of our beds with a mixture of entreaties and commands for 'silence'! We had little success. Having woken the household on three successive nights we moved him and his basket to the study which was below our bedroom, believing optimistically that then we would be the only disturbed dreamers. We survived only two nights of Jonnie's cries, and on the third night we brought him upstairs to the bathroom, which adjoined our bedroom. He never cried again and never made any attempt to get out of the bathroom until the door was opened in the morning. His friends were near and he was happy.

Jonnie had been selected for the film as there were several scenes in which the dog was required to play with the otter. Normally there is not a lot of love lost between these two species, but Jonnie—being rather an innocent tender-hearted type—was delighted at being asked to play with anything! Proper introductions between Jonnie and Dusky were made during our hours of contact time in the compound. First of all, just to be on the safe side, we let them look at each other from two adjoining compounds, but as there were no apparent reactions of fear, or aggression, from either of them, we decided not to delay the meeting any longer. Time was too precious and there was too little of it.

Contact time for Jonnie and Dusky was a never-ending, always-exciting game of hide-and-seek. With Dusky doing most of the hiding. The speed with which she humped her way across the ground surprised Jonnie even more than it surprised us. She would tear across the grass to where the land fell gently away towards the stream, sliding under bushes and through the rough grass, her direction constantly changing—leaving Jonnie springing hopefully in quite the wrong direction, his ears flying at right angles and his eyes wide with astonishment. When they finally met up they would play catch, or roll on their backs, revelling in the strange new companionship —obviously believing any second of stillness to be a second wasted.

Our director, Jack Couffer, a charming gentle person with many years of experience in animal films, as camera-man and director, came up to watch the two animals playing together, after hearing our enthusiastic reports on the progress being made. No one could have failed to be astonished, amused and touched by the behaviour of the dog and the otter—indeed, Jack was so delighted the next day he brought up a camera into the compound and filmed several hours of the animals playing together, watched by Bill and myself. Only a small proportion of this could be used in the film, but it was exceptional material, beautifully photographed.

CHAPTER SEVEN

Bambi

♣

WHEREVER we go we acquire animals. It is not really very difficult when you like them. When Jonnie had been with us at Muckairn for a week I knew I would find it impossible to part with him when the film was over. If I am honest I knew this when he had been at the house only one day, but I felt I should wait a reasonable time in order to be sure. So I waited a week. He belonged to a Mrs Thomson from Castle Douglas, from whom the film company had 'hired' him and from whom I bought him. Sometimes now at home he digs wildly in the flower-beds, uprooting precious, newly-planted flowers, or trips you up as you stagger down the path with armfuls of shopping, in his desire to express his joy at your being back after an absence of one whole hour; but his enthusiasm for life makes you forgive him immediately—well, after a minute or two!

It was not, however, only in his attitude to otters that Jonnie was somewhat unusual, but also to deer. Baby deer.

One day in June I was not called to work. I was pushing our youngest son, Daniel, down the driveway of Muckairn in his pram. It was a still peaceful afternoon, and I was enjoying being alone with the child and pointing out flowers and birds and butterflies. Suddenly a Land-Rover came driving towards us. I pushed the pram into the side of the road and, to my astonishment, the Land-Rover stopped and out got Neil, the farmer, with a tiny creature in his arms. 'Would you like to raise this?' he asked me. 'I found it in the woods.' I looked at this scrap of life and measured my ignorance of such things as rearing newly-born roe deer against its chances of survival if it were returned to the woods and, one hoped, re-accepted by its mother. Both situations seemed fairly desperate, but I knew that if it was not instantly reclaimed by the mother the likelihood of it living even one night was remote. 'Yes,' I said, 'I'll try.'

The most important things to find were a teat, a bottle and something to put in the latter. Neil gave me a teat he used for rearing lambs, we found a small beer bottle and then I set about trying to discover what to feed the little deer on. The veterinary in Oban did not know, but knew of someone who had raised a roe deer until it was several weeks old and gave me his telephone number. (He also advised me to come to the surgery and get some kind of antibiotic powder to put with the feed—when I knew what it was—as roe deer are prone to infection.) After some telephoning we decided to feed Bambi (as the children inevitably called him) on a very diluted mixture of cow's milk and glucose, to which we added the anti-biotic powder. The latter turned out to be pale green, and when mixed into the liquid the effect was rather exotic. We found a deep tea chest, lined it with straw, buried a hot water bottle wrapped in a towel well towards the bottom and installed Bambi in the kitchen recently vacated by Jonnie. If you have never seen a day-old roe deer you would find it hard to believe that anything so tiny could survive in nature's hard nursery. Tapering, pencil-slim legs rested on small polished hooves of incredible delicacy and supported a little spotted furry body. Vulnerable to almost everything, one would imagine. And yet Bambi was extremely strong and apparently very adaptable. The only cries we ever heard were just before feeding time; he seemed quite contented with his lot. He lost very little time in choosing a mother figure to replace his own—having known her for so little of his life perhaps he did not feel the loss too poignantly— and the object of his affections was none other than Jonnie. Jonnie was an excellent mother—he guarded Bambi and cleaned him up after meals and saw to it that he was always spick and span. When the deer grew a little bigger we used to take him into the sitting-room in the evening, and he would follow Jonnie along the passage, his little feet hardly imprinting the carpet as he picked his way to his favourite spot by the sofa. Even when Bambi tried to suck from Jonnie, the dog kept up the pretence with great strength of will, only his eyes betraying the confusion and surprise that he must have been feeling.

Only once did we have any problems with Bambi's health. For no apparent reason he suddenly became listless and dry-nosed and took no interest in his food. By now he was out in a pen in the garden during the day and grazing and browsing freely. Perhaps he had been poisoned by some plant? We telephoned the veterinary in Oban and he kindly came out to see Bambi—diagnosing the trouble immediately. It seems we should have discontinued the antibiotic powder after a week, and here we were at three weeks still using it! The result was that all the goodness that Bambi should have been absorbing from the green foodstuff he was eating was being destroyed by the antibiotic. He was given a short course of vitamin injections and we had no further worries.

In filming *Born Free* we had used, whenever possible, wire-netting fences to compound off the area in which we were working and so reduce the hazards of the animal straying and the problems of enticing it back towards the camera. At first it was not thought necessary to use this technique with otters, believing, perhaps, that they would be easy to catch and put back in position and that compounding would take time and cost money. Bill was most anxious that the fences should be erected—one only needed light portable sections on posts—so that the temptations of river, pools and seashore with its ribbons of shining seaweed would be temporarily out of reach. After a great deal of discussion fences were made and concentration, from both the otter's and actor's point of view, became better. Otter compounds. Swan compounds.

Sometimes we used to get up very early in the morning at Muckairn, before the sun had risen above the hills, but its cool yellow light was already diffusing the still surface of the loch. The pale morning air was crystal clear, embracing the happy flight of the oyster-catchers which skimmed the shore line. Sandy sandpipers picked their delicate way along the beach, catching the early worms—or whatever the equivalent is in the sandpipers' world. The first time we saw the two wild swans we could not quite believe it. When the beauty of the scene is so complete one sometimes needs to walk away from it. It is overwhelming. The two white birds glided across the water towards us, the path they cut making gentle ripples on either side of their bodies and causing the mountains in the loch surface to stir for a few quivering seconds. They graciously accepted the pieces of bread we had with us, and having eaten continued silently on their way. They became a familiar sight on those early morning walks, and I used to watch them with a particular interest, knowing that beneath their stately beauty lay a tremendous strength. A blow from a swan's wing can break a person's arm.

In the film I had to do a scene in which I walked fully dressed into the sea to rescue a baby cygnet whose leg was caught in some wire. The parent swans were to be there too, but I was assured there was no problem at all provided the adult swans used for the scene were not the real parents of the cygnet. The day arrived to do the scene and I went down to a small cove, where they had compounded off a part of the sea so that the swans could not swim away.

Standing on the shore were two large adult swans and beside them, in a large wire basket, five cygnets. The swans were the real parents of these cygnets. At such a time one can do absolutely nothing except hope that the swans will believe that you aren't a danger, you are not going to hurt the babies—one can hardly say to an entire film unit, poised for action, 'I'm sorry, I can't do

it, these are the cygnet's real parents!' So I waded into the
sea and into an unknown situation. The poor mother
simply could not understand what was going on—she
fussed around us, making hissing noises through her
black and yellow bill and puffing out her wings, all of
which combined to turn my already uncertain fingers
into bunches of unwieldy bananas. But that was all she
did—she made no attempt to attack me as I tried to un-
twist the piece of wire from around the little one's leg—
murmuring what I hoped were sounds of reassurance to
both mother and child. It all seemed to take a very long
time, but eventually I splashed back to the beach and the
swan family swam off a little way to calm their nerves.
Of course, we had to do it all over again—to get another
camera angle!

Swans, goslings and geese. Both Bill and Dusky had
to work with four downy goslings, enchanting little
creatures, light of foot and high of voice, who scurried
here and there in a perpetual game of follow-my-leader.
The adult geese behaved in a much more dignified
manner, gazing somewhat scornfully down their beaks
at the strange antics of their human companions.

No animal films are easy to make. Nearly everyone has
a different theory about how things should be done, and
influencing nearly everyone are the pressures of time and
money. But if you are making animal films in the way
that *Ring of Bright Water* was made, that *Born Free* was made
and that, later on, *An Elephant called Slowly* was made, if you
allow the animals to become friends and to behave
naturally it is difficult to impose schedules. If you are
not prepared to chain animals' feet to the ground,

sedate them, pull out their teeth and their claws and generally subscribe to a cruel domination, then you must accept the fact that possibly the film will take longer to make and that it will cost more money. I believe these facts must be accepted. Above and beyond any financial rewards the producers may reap from working in this way, are the immeasurable inner rewards most people connected with the film must surely receive. We should, before it is too late, care deeply about all the species in this world and have a 'reverence for all life' as Schweitzer said.

The work with the animals and with the people continued for four months. Four months of Scotland. Scotland—doesn't that word conjure up a wild beauty in your mind's eye? It is not only in Africa that the mountains are purple, that the clouds hang darkly in folds of violet and black. Here, too, paths dwindle into bush and heather and unimagined secrets hide behind the next hill. Water lies everywhere, repeating over and over again the beauty of the hills and the sky in its surface. Water falls everywhere, from gently bubbling burns to wide strong rivers, spilling over brown and grey rocks into foaming pools of darkness. The animals and birds have a difference too—the highland cattle with their long brown coats and seductive fringes, the thick-coated sheep grazing on the desolate moors, the red deer shy and elusive on the mountain side. They have, to my way of thinking, an untamed pride. Perhaps it stirs me so much because, like Africa, Scotland is still so untouched by man. One's soul can fly with the gulls and the terns.

The four months drew to a close and we had a very

difficult problem to solve. What should we do with Bambi? He was still too young to be set free in the forests, and even if this had not been the case it would not, I think, have been a wise thing to do. Bambi trusted people and many people shoot deer for sport. Again, the veterinary in Oban came to our assistance. He told me of a very remarkable man called Mr MacCaskill, the Head Forester at Inverinan. This was a densely wooded area up in the hills, not far from where we lived, and one afternoon the children and I went to visit him. The children were very concerned about Bambi and his future—they had always been very gentle with him, introducing him, when he was tiny, to the wonders of the garden and vying with each other to give him his bottle.

Mr MacCaskill was a very unusual man. He had a large garden at the back of his little house, in which he had at the time we met him the most intriguing collection of animals I have seen for a long time. A family of foxes, two red deer, a raven called Cronkie, two owls, a weasel, red and grey squirrels and quite a number of rabbits.

By a very strange coincidence, he had another roe deer of the same age as Bambi, a female called Gem. Mr MacCaskill's dream was to establish, alongside the beautiful forest walks which wind up the hills and mountains of Inverinan, some large fenced-off areas, each containing different species of deer. Deer, that is, indigenous to Britain. He already had his pair of red deer, and now, if we gave him Bambi, he would have his roe deer. We walked up the forest path to see the compound into which Bambi and Gem would ultimately go. It comprised ten acres—ten acres of trees and shrubs and ferns—almost of freedom. The animals could feed naturally during most of the year, but during the cold winter months their diet would be supplemented. It seemed ideal.

I believed very much in Mr MacCaskill, in his genuine concern for animals and their happiness. None of the animals or birds that he had were deliberately captured by him—only those found wounded or deserted or ill, or those belonging to people who could no longer care for them, were given sanctuary in his garden.

A few days later we took Bambi up to Inverinan and introduced him to Gem. Neither of them seemed particularly interested at first, but when we went up a few days later they appeared quite contented and I felt at ease about Bambi's future.

There were a lot of goodbyes to be said, to the kind and hospitable Scottish people we had met, so warm, direct—so real; and to the many animal friends we had made during our stay. We did not know, then, that there was a part of this Scottish adventure which was yet to be told. The tragic part. We were not to find out about that for quite some time.

In fact, it was the following year, in November, that Bill and I flew up to Edinburgh early one morning with our two elder sons William and Justin. The boys had two days' holiday for their half-term and we had decided that they should come with us to look over a prospective school. We took an early plane so that we could drive over to the west of Scotland, to Inverinan, to see Bambi, for it seemed impossible to visit Scotland without taking the opportunity of seeing him once again. Bambi would now be a year and a half, and from a photograph I had been sent I knew he was a beautiful animal, his first pair of horns standing proudly on his head. I knew we would not see Mr MacCaskill as he had been transferred to another area the previous summer. He had been able to take one or two of his animals with him, but had left the roe deer and the red deer to be looked after by the new Forester at Inverinan, Mr George Francey.

We landed in Edinburgh in a snowstorm. Huge, dense, swirling flakes transforming the colours of the earth, within seconds, into unbroken whiteness. As we drove along towards the west I sat in the front of the hired car, clutching a map, and adding to the difficulties of navigation caused by the windscreen constantly steaming up, by doing a more than usually inadequate job of map-reading. The roads along the south of the Firth of Forth didn't seem like Scotland. They continued endlessly through towns interspersed with only a few snatches of countryside. At last we were out into the open with the snowstorm behind us, the colours of autumn running wildly over the hills and trees which still waited patiently for their share of winter's gentle blanket.

Bill wanted to go for lunch to the Bailie Nicol Jarvie Hotel where we had once stayed—and spent an exhilarating evening joining in the Scottish reel dancing. We turned off the main road and twisted for several miles along country lanes, singing and chattering until we reached the hotel. It was closed! We should have guessed —summer was over, visitors were few and many hotels shut their doors during the winter months. We drove back, in silence, to Callander. It was now rather late, so we bought hot pies and rolls in a baker's shop which, as we were ravenous, tasted better than any hotel lunch.

We reached the main road to Oban as the skies were beginning to lower with heavy grey clouds. Up here the roads were partly covered with snow from an earlier fall, frozen solid, and driving was tricky and noisy as the hard pieces of snow flew up against the undercarriage of the car. The mist looped down and sleet washed the windscreen. We arrived at the eastern end of Loch Awe and debated whether we should turn back, as the journey had taken much longer than we anticipated. But we felt we had come too far not to go on.

As we got higher a sharp wind had blown the snow into drifts on the roadside and we now had only ice to contend with. We found ourselves at the Forestry hut at Inverinan at about 3.15 p.m. and I went into the little office where a man and a woman were working. I explained we had come to see Bambi who formerly belonged to us. 'Oh . . . you know that Gem is dead?' said the woman. I felt very sad. I had only seen her twice but I remembered how timid and delicate she had been. 'Yours is the other one, isn't it?' the woman asked. 'Yes,' I said, 'Bambi, the male.' At this point Bill came into the room with the children and she continued in her soft Highland accent, 'Have you not got boots? The path up there is terrible, your feet will get awful wet.' 'We've come a long way,' I said, determined not to be put off, 'and we can't leave without seeing him,' I added firmly.

We left the hut and climbed the stony forest path which was, in places, a fast-flowing icy stream. The boys rolled up the bottom of their trousers and we splashed and shivered up the path, paying little attention to our wet feet. All our concentration was on reaching the compound and seeing Bambi. When we got to the lower end of the wire netting we began to call his name, but nothing had appeared by the time we reached the top end and had walked down the side towards his shelter and feeding place. I left Bill and the children at that side and went back a short way down the track, peering through the wire into the little dark wood. 'There he is!' I heard Justin's voice behind me. I looked round and there, through the trees, the shadowy shape of a deer was moving quickly towards the top end of the enclosure. I was overjoyed. We stumbled back up the path, but just as I turned the corner the animal sped past me down the length of the hill and disappeared. We stood and softly called for about ten more minutes, but he didn't show himself again, and as we turned to retrace our slippery way we saw a man coming up the path towards us. It was Mr Francey the Head Forester. We introduced ourselves and I told him that we had seen Bambi twice. 'Oh yes,' he said rather unenthusiastically, 'have you not heard from Mr MacCaskill?' 'No,' I replied. His face was pale. 'It is not Gem who is dead,' he said, 'it is Bambi.'

I felt stunned. Mechanically, I went with the others as they moved down the path, but I could not follow the conversation because my head was teeming with memories of Bambi. We said goodbye to Mr Francey and we drove, speaking little, the sixty-five miles to Crieff, where we had decided to spend the night. The children were almost asleep at dinner and were only too pleased to get into bed. Anticipating the comfort of warm sheets, I unpacked a few things and talked quietly to Bill about Bambi. He had hardly said a word, but was looking at me with such a strange smile on his face. I stopped and looked at him, I knew what that look meant—forgive me, but I must tell you something that will hurt you. I don't want to but I must.

'There is something which Mr Francey told me, something that you don't know,' Bill said quietly. 'When Bambi was found, both his horns had been cut off.' My blood ran cold. I stared at Bill not believing I had heard him correctly. 'What do you mean?' 'Both horns had been taken off.' 'But why,' I asked, 'didn't Mr Francey tell me this?' 'I think he didn't want to distress you.' Bill then told me the story as told to him by the Forester. Early that morning two stalkers had seen the two deer playing at the lower end of the compound. The stalkers had then gone to shoot on the other side of the mountain. Later in the morning two women visitors reported that while walking by the pen they had noticed that one of the deer was lying rather still. Mr Francey told Bill that as he did not feel a particular cause for alarm, he did not go up to the compound until 2.15 p.m. He found the deer lying there. It was Bambi—dead. His horns had been cut off above the coronet. A cast horn, of probably a previous year, was lying nearby, but there was no trace of Bambi's horns. According to Mr Francey, horns cut off in this way have no value—those prized as trophies are taken off below the coronet. There was no sign of a struggle. There were no footprints. The ground was dry.

Bill said he had questioned Mr Francey further. The

body of Bambi had been sent to the veterinary school at Oban to have an autopsy performed. The verbal report gave worms as the cause of death—a secondary infection from dogs or foxes. Mr Francey stated that the animal had not been in contact with dogs, but foxes were another matter. Mr MacCaskill had had a family of foxes in the garden behind his house and later they spent some time in a small compound within the large one belonging to the deer.

'But why, then, were the horns removed?' I asked Bill. 'Mr Francey could give no explanation,' Bill replied.

Questions posed themselves at every corner. There seemed to me, as I lay in bed in the morning waiting for light to seep through the curtains, two possibilities. The first was that someone walking past had noticed the animal lying still, had got into the compound—either climbed into it or opened the gate with a key—and on finding Bambi dead had decided to remove the horns, either with an instrument he carried, or with one he went away to collect. This seemed far-fetched. The second possibility was more unpleasant. That someone had deliberately gone to the compound equipped with a saw and removed Bambi's horns while he was still alive. This action might have been the cause of death (although death might not have been intended) if Bambi had been very ill and had struggled violently, but why, I asked myself, would anyone want to do such a thing? I knew that hand-reared roe buck can become extremely danger- ous, but would anyone take such drastic measures out of fear for themselves or their family? It seemed incon- ceivable. But one thing was certain. Either before or after death someone had seen fit to mutilate Bambi.

I suggested to Bill that we leave early and, having visited the school, we contacted Mr MacCaskill before taking the plane back. It meant a drive of a couple of hours, but by now I could not leave the mystery of Bambi's death to further speculation. We arrived at Queen's View, where Mr MacCaskill lived, and I told him we had been to Inverinan the previous day. I think it was a shock to Mr MacCaskill. He said that he had not written to tell me of Bambi's death because, although he had tried, he had not been able to put pen to paper. Now he felt very badly that I had found out in this way. He was not at all convinced Bambi's death was caused by worms. He believed as I did that Bambi's horns had been removed deliberately and that he might have died of shock, although the veterinary had said that the horns had been removed after death because of the small amount of blood flow.

We left Scotland, but on the plane I was only more uncertain than ever as to what had really happened. As we flew over the industrial Midlands and saw the concentration of lights below, which revealed the unwieldy spires and heaps of foundries and factories, I asked myself would we ever find out the truth about Bambi? And as I thought of the masses of humanity crowded into the factory towns, people for whom forest walks and rivers and the sound of the sea were perhaps little known phenomena, I wondered whether I was right to care so much. Whether or not I was right, I knew that it was a problem that, until it was solved, would disturb me from time to time for the rest of my life. Somewhere there is a person who knows why the horns were cut off, who knows his own fear.

I have been somewhat comforted by a further report from the veterinary in Oban of the autopsy. It appears that thrombosis was the real cause of death accompanied by peritonitis. His end must have come very quickly.

The mystery still to be solved is why and by whom his horns were removed. As long as man's fear remains I doubt that it ever will be.

CHAPTER EIGHT

'Is This What Being a Filmstar Means?'

♣

FROM Muckairn we were not coming home empty-handed—we were bringing Jonnie. We wondered very much what kind of reception he would receive from Nell and from Boy—the oldest inhabitant. We needn't have worried about Nell—being of opposite sexes they got on like a house on fire, but in the case of Boy it was a different matter. Boy felt not a little put out by the intrusion of this noisy newcomer, and Jonnie suddenly found himself having to share our time and affection instead of being the object of our undivided attention. It was hard for both of them to accept this new situation, and though now they treat each other with an unwilling tolerance, occasionally the fire bubbling underneath will break through and the air will resound with a symphony of growls and barks and general disapproval. Poor Macduff, the cat, had rather a rough time for the first few weeks—Jonnie had really no experience of cats, certainly not at such consistently close quarters, and the temptation to chase a waving black tail was too much. He has, over the months, become a little more restrained, and Macduff has developed great expertise in the art of evasion and even avoidance.

Muckairn

It was lovely to be home again. The children ran excitedly from room to room, discovering once-discarded toys and gathering them in their arms with reawakened enthusiasm. The garden echoed with their shouts as swings were swung upon and the long 'tarzan rope' that hangs from a massive high-branched oak carried them in turn to momentary obscurity among the leaves.

There is a particular freedom one feels in one's own territory—familiar but no less precious for being so. The scent of the woods, cool and fern-green, or smelling of damp leaf-soaked earth, after the English summer rains. This is the kind of inheritance we should leave our children. An awareness of beauty, a sense of involvement with all life, a tenderness towards everything in one's care. These riches, unlike money, can remain with us all our lives.

Bill, during the weeks of summer, had been quietly scribbling notes and thinking. He was preoccupied, and I didn't ask too many questions, as I know he believes that if one discusses embryonic thoughts and ideas before they are formed, before they are tangible, one can hurt these ideas, stultify them. They will never grow. They are already secondhand.

He told me, one morning in September, that he was writing a story for a film about Africa—about elephants in Africa—about a couple who go to Africa to live with elephants, to learn about elephants. 'It's more of a comedy this time,' Bill said. 'Who is the couple who go to Africa?' I asked (somewhat foolishly as I afterwards realized). 'Us,' Bill replied.

We are flying at 36,000 feet and below us is Africa.

Behind us, and only yesterday, are our home and our children.

Already a memory are the soft English fields and woods, holding secrets of life we foolishly explore too seldom because we live amongst them and feel, mistakenly, that we know them.

Below us is the unknown—limitless miles of wilderness, dun-coloured whispering grasses baked and bleached by the sun. Dense, dark luxuriant forests undiscovered by that same sun—tangles of vine and creeper twisting and caressing the mammoth trunks of trees and lacing the heavy air. Both wilderness and forest hold secrets, and these we long to investigate, to enquire into the nature of their being and in so doing enlighten the nature of our own.

Plant life, insect and bird and animal—we can only touch the surface of creation. Bill and I have come rather late in our lives to this conscious awareness of the animal kingdom and our own human insignificance in the over-all pattern of existence. A vast new world has been opened up before us—a world with a confusing number of roads to follow, all marked by signposts which inspire the imagination. Struggle for survival. Minority groups. Conservation. Ecology. We are neither zoologists nor scientists nor any kind of experts on animal life. We are, basically, actors who, because of our work in recent years, have had personal contact with certain undomesticated species of animals. We were fascinated. We are now involved. Man's inhumanity to man is an old theme. That it still exists, and increasingly so, is an unhappy reflection on the nature of man. The relentless materialism of the world which we have made for ourselves increases our intolerance and hardens our ambitious hearts against humanitarian behaviour. This is left to our charities and our benevolent societies. Man's inhumanity to animals has always been accepted. If we can be cruel to each other, why should our conscience be touched by similar behaviour towards so-called inferior creatures?

We would like to make it impossible for there to be a world where elephants' feet are made into umbrella stands; handbags are covered with the flat grimacing faces of leopards; where the cries of seals being slaughtered in their thousands, and sometimes skinned before the last desperate breath, echo in the cold northern skies; where one may hear the baying of the hounds that pursue the otter and the fox to their violent end.

The violence of nature, the slaughter of the antelope by the lion—this we can accept because the reason behind the action is survival. The bravado of humans with firearms—killing not for survival but to prove superiority, manliness, and even for fun—with an end result of a skin rug or a mounted head—this in our world of vanishing wild creatures has no justification. We do not need now to kill wild animals in order that we can survive. We do not need their skins to keep us warm. We need, now, to let them live.

In a few moments we will be arriving in Nairobi. We do not know what the next five weeks hold in store for us—all we know is that we have come to make a film about elephants. About humans and elephants. About relationships. We have come to explore the dark forests.

The speed with which we now can travel from one

place to another makes it very difficult for us to arrive in a different country with any degree of adjustment or relaxation. We leave our homeland with its comparatively familiar customs, language and climate and nine hours later we are plunged into a completely strange scene. I have not been to the Far East, but I would imagine that the impact of the differences between their way of life and our way of life in Europe is equal to that which one experiences when arriving in Africa. Returning to East Africa this time was also, for me, an emotional revisiting. Ten of the most important months of my life had been spent here, and the country contained many places and many people who meant a great deal to me. Quite unexpectedly, one of these people was waiting to meet us at the airport. Standing at the barrier was George Adamson. There was too much to say to say anything.

Our little party consisted of James Hill, who was to direct our film, and Colin Jobson, a friend from our local town. He had his own camera shop, but was interested in finding out something about film-making, about all the machinations behind the scenes, and had agreed to come along and help in any way he could. He became an invaluable addition to the team, and no errand, however strange and unlikely it seemed, proved too difficult for him. We divided up into two groups and James and Colin went off to the New Stanley Hotel and Bill and myself to the house of Monty and Hilary Ruben, whom we had first met in 1964 and who had since become very warm and hospitable friends. Monty was to be an associate producer on our film.

We lost very little time in starting to make arrangements. We could not afford to. The short rains were neither far off nor predictable, so neither time nor money could be wasted. We arrived on a Wednesday; on Thursday we gathered together our equipment and clothes and on Friday we started filming—at the airport. Our cameraman, Simon Trevor, was a very sympathetic, hardworking young man, who had been a game warden, knew a great deal about wild life and in particular elephants. He had already been filming for us in the bush for several weeks, and we had been very impressed by his camerawork. By his dramatic style. He was a creative cameraman and his knowledge of animal behaviour allowed him to anticipate their movements—thereby capturing moments which might have eluded a less experienced person. He was married to an extremely charming Danish girl, Laila, who was not only a great help to him, but to us all.

Our sound man was Mike Richmond. He recorded everything on his Nagra, and we ignored such things as trucks roaring past and planes taking off—the nightmares of the sound operator—as we were going to have to record all the dialogue again back in London under, from a 'sound' point of view, more ideal conditions.

The first day on any film is never easy. People are unfamiliar with each other, perhaps with their equipment, with the story and with the conditions under which they are working. It is a tentative day and often has to be done again. We had a rather complicated dialogue scene to do with an Indian gentleman which, rather surprisingly, we managed to complete. This was largely due, I

73

think, to the Indian gentleman himself, who arrived ideally dressed for the part, no detail overlooked, and gave a performance of equal style. We were most fortunate.

The problems of amassing equipment, arranging locations, obtaining permissions, organizing our departure in a week's time to the Lake Manyara Park in Tanzania where we were to stay, inside the park itself, for several days—these problems were all overshadowed by one. It was vital to find a very young 'human-tolerating' elephant. It was essential that Bill and I should be able to establish a close relationship with this elephant which, in the story, was to adopt us. This achieved, we could then go into the other part of the story which was to study the behaviour and needs of the wild herds in order to suitably care for our own small friend. Without this firm background the point of the whole film was lost. It is not as easy as you might imagine to find a small, 'tame' elephant in Africa. In fact, our trip had been cancelled and re-booked more than once as each elephant that was found turned out to be the wrong age or unwell. Only two days before our departure did we receive a telegram telling us that one had definitely been found. How 'tame' it was we did not know. We were soon to find out. And other things besides. We had heard that it was two years old and that it had been caught some weeks ago. These statements we subsequently learned to be untrue—it was nearer four than two and had been caught only about ten days before. Its ultimate destination was the London Zoo, to whom the Kenya Government was presenting it as a gift. The elephant was loaned to us on condition that we replaced it should there be some mis-adventure.

We visited the little elephant late on Thursday after-noon. She was being held in a small compound at John Seago's—himself an animal trapper, but not responsible for the capture of this elephant. His particular methods of trapping were humane (if one allows any capturing of animals to be described in this way) and his animals were well cared for during the period he kept them in the holding enclosures prior to their departure for their various destinations. Unfortunately, these destinations were sometimes less happy than the enclosures he him-self was offering them.

We walked slowly down past the other animals stand-ing or lying patiently in their compounds. Mr Seago pointed out one rhino, lying quietly on its side. 'This would never be seen in the wild,' he told me. 'The animal is trusting and content.' I have heard of children and even adults seeking escape from reality in simu-lated sleep.

In the last compound we saw a small tense grey shape pacing nervously from one side of the solidly fenced pen to the other. As we came nearer it reversed towards the far end and then charged violently towards us, pulling up just short of the barricade. This was our 'tame' ele-phant. We stayed for some time next to the compound, hoping she would calm down as she became used to us and our voices. The nearest we got to any contact was to offer her some leafy branches, which she did take from us, charging towards us at great speed and tearing them from our hands. We felt concerned to say the least. We arranged with Mr Seago that someone should stay near the animal all the time, talking to it and, hopefully, establishing contact with it. We should visit it whenever our schedule permitted and it should have as much association with humans as possible. Kindly association. Obviously, until now, the elephant's experience of human beings had been most disturbing. At this point we could only rely on time and the right approach.

We had five days in which to do all the scenes in Nairobi. They were not easy. For the scene in which we were sitting in the aeroplane on our way to Kenya we obtained permission to film it actually flying in an aeroplane—a rather unusual procedure—as we felt some added effect might be gained by doing it realistically. From that point of view it was rather disappointing, and we spent a feverish time trying to get everything finished in the one hour's journey from Nairobi to Dar-es-Salaam. Matters were further complicated by the film lamps proving to be totally inadequate, and we had to rely mainly on natural light coming through the windows!

On arriving at Dar-es-Salaam, we went to a very nice hotel, the Kilimanjaro, ate a delicious lunch and then collapsed beside the swimming pool for a few hours, before catching our return flight to Nairobi. No experience is wasted, but from the point of view of the film we did not really add the extra atmosphere we had hoped for. One rather delightful moment occurred during our return trip. The air hostess was taking orders for drinks from a passenger in front of us for whom English was not a familiar tongue. 'Scotland and ginger ale, please,' the

Elephant in Manyara

gentleman said. The air hostess looked faintly puzzled. 'You know Scotland, don't you?' the passenger asked rather witheringly. 'Yes, Sir,' replied the hostess, and wrote down his order.

Monday's work did not involve technical problems, but diplomatic ones. We had to film a scene in a curio shop—the type that sells objects made from skin and ivory and leather and also displays an assortment of stuffed animal heads, gazing in perpetual dismay from the walls of their unchosen home. The scene required that I should go into the shop to buy postcards for the children and the shopkeeper had to try and discourage me from this modest purchase in the hope I would select one of the sad trophies (not sad to him, of course). We outlined the context of the scene to the Indian proprietor, who was most co-operative and anxious to please. I do not think he fully appreciated the implication of the scene. The morning was rather a strain. When we went to see the 'rushes' we saw that the lighting for the interior of the shop was inadequate and we realized we would have to do the scene again. We approached the proprietor but found him much less agreeable. He told us he had been informed by a white hunter that our film was against hunting and that the particular scene in his shop would ruin his business. Naturally he felt concerned. We were quite frank with him—we were against hunting, we said, especially for trophies and luxury goods and amusement. Not against him personally. It was all very difficult, but he eventually, rather reluctantly, allowed us to film the scene again. A gentle-eyed giraffe, sawn off at the base of the neck, watched our human antics from its resting place on the floor of the shop. To my disappointment, because of length, the scene was cut out of the film. It had made a point.

On Tuesday we were already having to plan for the time when we would come back from Lake Manyara. Our little elephant was constantly in our minds, and we were trying to find a location where we could film the close contact scenes with her. We had originally thought of Meru—where George was with the lions—but the journey was long and hard by road and might prove still more unsettling for the animal. We also had to have a small house, and although the Game Warden of Meru and his wife, Peter and Sarah Jenkins, had been most co-operative about the whole situation, we felt we could not really impose ourselves, an elephant and an undisciplined schedule upon them for two whole weeks.

Then someone mentioned Tsavo, and David Sheldrick. *The Orphans of Tsavo*, written by his wife, Daphne, is a fascinating, personal account of their life together in Tsavo National Park and the wild orphaned animals they have gathered round them over the years—some to stay, some to return to the wild. By a strange coincidence, David happened to be in Nairobi that day and we all met in Monty Ruben's office. We felt rather dubious about his reaction to us all coming to Tsavo and filming there. We had no proper script to show him, only some scribbled notes, and he had to take a lot on trust. For some reason he did. He said we could come to Tsavo and bring the elephant—plus the inevitable confusion that accompanies even a very small film unit.

For me, David Sheldrick is to elephants what George

Adamson is to lions. He is a deep-thinking, understanding man of great integrity. He and his warm and lovely wife are rare people in this world. The orphans that they had at this time were two elephants, three rhino and three buffalo, and a family of ostriches. One of the elephants was Eleanor—the little elephant we had used in *Born Free*, now almost eleven years old. David suggested we should fly down to Tsavo that afternoon, look at the location and see the animals, because he had no objection to our using them in the film. We flew in a small Aztec six-seater plane. The flight was rather bumpy. James hates small planes, Simon was ill and I very nearly was. All three of us were more than relieved to see the landing strip below with its reception committee of two ostriches! The earth in Tsavo is red—thousands of terra-cotta miles. It is an enormous park of dramatic beauty and huge elephants— the biggest elephants in Africa we are told. Someone met us at the plane and we drove a short distance through the park to our prospective camping site. Three makuti (palm frond) covered, whitewashed bandas stood on the edge of the bush. Two were deserted but the third pre-sented an almost unbelievable sight. In front of the little house was a garden—a riot of nasturtiums, marigolds, zinnias, geraniums, beautifully tended and surrounded by a low thorn fence—to keep out the dik-dik. Beside the banda was a large green bus. Inside the bus were two beds, a cooker, a fridge, cupboards—it was, in fact, a travelling home. All these wonders belonged to a delight-ful middle-aged couple called Mavis and Philip Hucks. They both had a deep love and understanding of life in the bush and were engaged in a completely voluntary study of the botanical life of Tsavo on behalf of Kenya Parks. They would load up their bus and go off into the bush for two to four weeks at a time. Self-contained. Content. They very kindly said we might film in front of their house and in the interior of their bus. For the interior of the house we would use one of the other empty bandas. We would have liked to talk longer, but we had to be back in Nairobi before nightfall. So we went off to see if we could find the orphans grazing somewhere in the bush in the care of their herdsman. Simon who, having worked here, knew the park and the orphans well, guided us to a likely spot and sure enough there were the rhinos, Rufus, Ruedi—blind in one eye, and Stub the baby—the elephants Eleanor and Kadenge, who was not an orphan but had been brought in from the bush five or six years before by Samson—another of the elephant orphans, since returned to the wild—and the three buffalo. It was an extraordinary situation and felt quite unreal. Here we were in the African bush walking about stroking fully grown rhino and fairly impressive elephants! If only this could be reality—co-existence—a world without mutual fear. I felt very excited at the idea of coming back to Tsavo to work and live with these animals.

We had one more day's work in Nairobi, a hot, rather frustrating day, filming inside an aeroplane which was itself inside a hangar, having its routine service. Uniformed officials and workmen were going in and out carrying seats and equipment—trays of food that we had arranged to be ready for the scene never turned up. James began to quiver. 'Control,' he said masterfully, 'we'll scrap that scene and have drinks instead.' The interior of the plane was very hot and patience was dwindling fast. One rather provocative Indian girl who was playing the part of one of the passengers was obviously finding the whole business most disillusioning. 'Is this what being a filmstar means?' she asked. 'One day of this and I'd go potty,'

CHAPTER NINE

On the Shores of Lake Manyara

♣

AT last the work in the city was, for the moment, over. Not being town dwellers, we found it very hard to attune ourselves to the noise and pressures of urban life. We were aching to get out into the wild, and when at about 8.30 on Thursday morning we loaded up our Land-Rover with an incredible amount of equipment and supplies and set off, in convoy, with Simon's Toyota and Mike's VW Microbus to Lake Manyara, we felt an immense surge of relief.

At this point I think I should say a word or two more about our Land-Rover, which once upon a time must have been a most beautiful and efficient motor car. We called it Mr Mopagee—the name of the Indian gentleman in the story with whom we had played the scene at the airport. Mr Mopagee was painted in dazzling but dirty stripes of yellow and black. It had no windscreen and only half a roof. These inconveniences we accepted as they were necessary to the character of the vehicle in the film. That it had other deficiencies was revealed to us all too soon on our journey to Tanzania. It had absolutely no springs and dust seeped through every hole and chink until we both looked like strange pale ghosts, prematurely grey. The noise of Mopagee's vibrations as we shook mercilessly over the hard, corrugated road resounded in our heads and deafened us to all but the most penetrating sounds. Perhaps we could have accepted—although it was a lot to ask—the dust and the vibrations and our bruised and battered bodies, but when the speed slowly dropped from a hair-raising fifty miles per hour to a steady fifteen, and we knew we had 248 miles before us, our tolerance dwindled noticeably. When the engine stopped altogether we were speechless. True, we had asked for a disreputable, crazy-looking Land-Rover with a character of its own, but we were only referring to its appearance, not to its inner workings! Bill managed to get it started again, and after one or two more stops we lurched into a village garage. I strolled up and down the hot street while a few Masai peered into the engine and made discouraging noises. After about twenty minutes and a lot of clinking of tools and revving of engine, we climbed back into our seats and resumed our journey. This was the first of many such incidents with Mr Mopagee. It seemed that its engine reached boiling point before the engines of most cars have even warmed up! It was not comforting knowledge.

We reached the park itself at 5.45 that evening—it was dusk—having stopped in Arusha for a very pleasant lunch with John Owen and his wife. He was the head of Tanzania Parks and he showed us great hospitality and kindness. No one is allowed to camp inside the park except scientists and assistants, but Mr Owen had given us permission to stay at the Research Camp used by Ian Douglas Hamilton, who was making a study of elephant.

As we drove through the park gates, the visitors were coming out and we knew that apart from ourselves and a few game rangers we were alone with the animals. It was a new sensation. Very elating. We drove slowly through the park, alert for any signs of animal life, and wound our way up an escarpment to the half-dozen white bandas which formed the camp. Two or three rangers were there, and we explained who we were and that we were staying for a few days. (Ian Douglas Hamilton was away in England at the time.) We got the calor gas working and lit the lamps and the stove, and Laila and I unpacked the food and got a meal while the men sorted out the camera equipment and erected the two tents. Simon and Laila and Mike were sleeping under canvas and Bill and I were to use Ian Douglas Hamilton's banda—the one highest up the escarpment and about 120 yards from the main building where we ate and worked. We were all tired. The journey had been long and dusty and we felt like going to bed in preparation for an early start the next morning. Bill and I gathered together our paraphernalia—lamp, Thermos of boiled water for doing our teeth, towels, suitcase—and clutching it all untidily in our arms we started slowly up the uneven, rocky path. We had gone only fifty yards when something coughed in the bushes on our right. I nearly jumped out of my skin and backed into Bill, who was just behind me. 'Did you hear that?' I asked, rather unnecessarily. 'Yes,' Bill replied calmly. 'It's probably only a lion. There's really no need to feel alarmed. After all, it's used to people going up and down the path.' In the face of such cool logic I felt somewhat unreasonable and had to content myself with feverish mutterings to give myself encouragement to climb the remaining distance to our bedroom, grasping at slipping towels and Thermos with trembling hands. I have never known such a short walk to take so long. Actually I felt rather foolish about the whole business and was most relieved when I had a chance to 'save Bill's life' only a few moments later. Well, it seemed like that at the time and I needed the chance to vindicate myself. We reached the safety of the banda and started to get ready for bed. 'I think there's a cater-pillar or something inside my trousers,' Bill said casually. He took them off and shook them and a shiny creature dropped on to the floor and scurried past my feet, waving at us menacingly. Instinctively I put my foot on it. For-tunately I was still wearing my shoes, and when we got the lamp and inspected it closely we saw a small, olive-green scorpion of a particularly poisonous variety. From then on we always wore shoes—except when we were actually in bed! We reported both incidents to the rest of the company next morning, and they were greeted with much laughter. Simon informed me that it would have been a leopard that made such a coughing sound— we examined the track for footprints and sure enough found several feline traces on and beside the path. Con-sidering all this, and the fact that Bill might have been prostrate from a scorpion bite, I took a somewhat dim view of the laughter! From then on I always waited for Bill before climbing the path at night.

The camp was in a very beautiful setting. Nestling into the steep side of the escarpment, it looked down on a wide river to which animals of all kinds came to drink.

Particularly elephant. The water fell in a roaring cascade just above our banda over the rocks to the river below. Around us and beyond the river was the wilderness of the park.

We decided not to do any filming with the elephant herds the first morning, but to drive near them and watch them. It was quite alarming suddenly to find oneself only a few yards away from these prehistoric giants—especially as one was still unfamiliar with their behaviour pattern and inclined to misinterpret most of the things they did. We had always believed that when elephant flapped their ears it meant they were angry. This is not so. Dispersed over the ear flap is an intricate network of veins and arteries which act as a cooling apparatus. The constant movement of the ears speeds up the cooling process. When they are angry their ears do, indeed, stand out, but rigid and tense, expressing the animals' aggressive intent. We also believed that every time an elephant made a rush towards you it meant business. Well, in a way it did, but not always of an uncompromisingly serious nature. If the trunk was up it was only 'making a show'. Warning you. When the trunk was down, and the tusks were then levelled towards you, that was the time to disappear from the scene.

So many things astonished us. The speed with which the elephant advanced through the undergrowth, the silence with which they moved. Vast grey phantoms, their presence was often only revealed by the low rumblings in their throats and nasal passages. No one really knows the significance of this rumbling sound, but it is believed to be some form of communication. We heard it among elephant in their wild state and we also heard our own elephant make it, between each other and to us. How I wished I could interpret it.

Living in the wild has an extraordinary value. One is aware of the life of the creatures around one and of one's own life with an unaccustomed degree of perception. Every action and thought has a direct importance, and our senses become sharpened because of this. Perhaps it is, in a way, similar to the awareness which we developed when we made *Born Free*. When life and the possibility of death are so close together, nothing can be wasted, neither new knowledge nor new disillusionment. Everything is precious.

Death and decay lie exposed before you in the wild. A limp white egret, its slender body distorted by the unfriendly thorn bush which suspended it above the pool, the massive dark rotting body of the buffalo already half hidden by the vultures and the Maribou storks as they consumed their ghoulish but necessary feast. Undisguised extinction. And there is birth too, innocent and vulnerable. The new born in the wild, from gazelle to elephant, must fight its own battle for survival from the moment it opens its eyes on its strange, untrodden world. There is no comfortable gap between a first and an ultimate breath.

As we had dreamed lions on the boat going out to make *Born Free*, so we now dreamed elephants. We asked endless questions, we watched the immensely powerful yet graceful animals as they stripped trees of their branches and their bark, and sprayed themselves with water and mud down at the river, or moved quietly through the forest in their search for food. The need for food was never-ending—an adult elephant must consume about 500 pounds of food a day and drink approximately 30 gallons of water.

The sun was yellowing and sinking low in the sky as we started to drive back to camp at the end of our first day at Manyara. Suddenly a shrill scream pierced the still air, and behind some trees on our left there resounded a great commotion of animals thrashing through the undergrowth, branches of trees and bushes being torn and trampled upon indiscriminately as the creatures moved about in uncontrollable emotion. The screams and trumpeting continued and within seconds a group of alarmed and nervous elephant streamed across the road only a few yards beyond our vehicles. They moved into the bush on the other side of the road and after only a few moments all was quiet. We never discovered the cause of the disturbance, but Simon thought it might have been a leopard. This was our first experience of group agitation. The second, which occurred on our last day in the park, was on a very much larger scale. It was early in the morning and we had been filming with a large herd of elephant which was grazing near the road and only a short distance from a herd of impala. Again there was a sudden piercing trumpeting and screaming, and the whole vast herd turned in unison and moved urgently and silently across the road and into the bush on the right, the white dust spraying up around their legs and almost concealing the younger members of the group. The trumpeting this time, however, did not stop—it just became fainter as the animals penetrated deeper into the forest, and by the time the bull appeared, his huge frame tense and dangerous as he moved with incredible speed after the others, it had become an almost inaudible echo in the far distance. We had managed to film the stampede and now drove after Simon as he skilfully anticipated the next position where the herd would break into the open. We stopped on a piece of high ground which overlooked a clearing on the edge of the forest, and sure enough, a few minutes later, a large part of the herd appeared, travelling at an even greater speed and with no lessening of agitation. A large cow elephant sensed our presence and looked up at us, her tusks pointing at us. Simon said if we had been on the same ground level and nearer to her we would have had to make a fast retreat. I felt I would have needed little encouragement! Again we never discovered the cause of the stampede, but one or two of the rangers with whom we spoke later that day said they thought it might have been caused by bees swarming.

It was usually during our encounters with smaller groups or even individual elephant, who quite often were rather annoyed at being disturbed, that Mr Mopagee decided to reach boiling-point. Bill and I always had a lengthy debate when we were in a good position for Simon to film us with the elephants, as to whether we should leave the engine running and risk it boiling over and stalling—thereby making us a sitting target for any unwelcoming animal—or switch the engine off and risk not being able to start it again. The choice was fairly depressing! We usually decided on the latter course, and on more than one occasion our fears were realized and

Mr Mopagee emitted nothing but a few despairing wheezes. Luckily for us, the elephants must have realized we were rather at a loss and never made things too unpleasant—apart from one occasion when we had driven up very close to a thick clump of bamboo from which the sounds of two elephants having a violent disagreement were issuing. I wasn't too happy about sitting there so conspicuously in Mr Mopagee—after all, no one could say his yellow and black stripes presented even a suggestion of camouflage—but it seemed a pity to waste what might be a good shot for the film.

Bill switched off the engine and we sat there listening to the shrill argument and anticipating just about every possible subsequent situation. We did not have to wait very long. The bamboo crashed open and there, a few yards in front of us, was an irate young bull. My hands were sweating so much I might have been washing them in running water! And I felt no more relaxed when the elephant defied us, making several mock charges in our direction. Simon told us afterwards that they were mock, but at the time there didn't seem very much difference between mock and real! We held our ground—there wasn't really very much option as even if we had been able to start Mr Mopagee it wasn't exactly the car in which to make a quick getaway—and after a few more baleful glances the bull must have decided we presented no real threat and turned and disappeared from view.

Not all our experiences of elephant were dramatic or fearful. We spent many absorbing hours following the herds as they went to the river for water—watching them resting in the shade of the palms, the babies lying on their sides, tired from the heat of the sun and from the long distances they must travel to keep up with the herd. The fascination of watching the elephant in a 'wallow'—a large muddy pool of water in which they roll, splash, spray themselves and appear to be very delighted with life. They seem to do all this both to cool their skins and also to cover their skins with the mud as a protection from insects.

It was often while we were waiting, in position, for elephant to appear at a wallow or a river that we observed the other inhabitants of the park. Whether it was because our eldest son, William, has a deep interest in and some knowledge of birds, stemming from our stay in Kenya in 1964, I do not know, but on this visit I became very much more conscious of the feathered life in the wild. In particular I remember one day, rather late in the afternoon, when we were waiting near the edge of the lake itself, and beside a sandy-banked river to which we hoped the herd would come for water (in fact it stayed further upstream and never appeared!). A Kittlitz sand plover splashed and bathed contentedly in the shallow water and three Egyptian geese swooped, honking, to land near us on the still lake. An immature stilt picked its way delicately along the edge of the sand—a peaceful, gentle scene, backed by the fierce splendour of a Batteleur eagle and a fish eagle, sitting on opposite ends of a fallen dead tree. The park is filled with exotic and unusual birds, one of my favourite being the coucal, a brown bird with a long tail and little ability to fly, with the charming nickname of the 'water bottle bird'—a name which aptly describes the noise it makes. Saddle bills, sacred ibis, hornbills, storks—yellow-billed and hammer-headed—egrets which follow the buffalo on whom they depend so largely for their existence (the buffalo hooves churn up the ground and disturb the innumerable insect inhabitants which form part of the egrets' diet), and the charming, dignified pelican swimming in their clusters of cool, yet glaring, whiteness on the edge of the shallow waters of Lake Manyara. Its water was dazzling under the midday sun, and we used to seek shelter from its restless brilliance in the forest world of undertones and shadows. A world of soothing quietness and yet where the sound of a leaf falling might have another meaning. Our untrained eyes saw little—a few monkeys and birds—but we were, I am sure, being watched by the sensitive eyes of many other forest dwellers.

Only a year ago the moon was still a distant world of mystery, which stirred the imagination and had been a source of inspiration to poets throughout generations. The virgin goddess, Diana, still hunted in its silvery light and the 'man in the moon' held unshaken power within the freedom of our fantasy. At Manyara the moon rose from behind the umbrella trees—a huge apricot-golden sphere, simulating a night-sun in the dark blue tropical sky. Could it really be the moon—was it only the veil of dust between it and the sun which gave it this superb and unreal aura? Or was the 'man in the moon' stoking some hidden fiery furnace in the unexplored depths of his cold kingdom? Now we can no longer weave our illusions. Theories have become facts. We know that Diana and her maidens have vanished forever and that nothing can survive in the lifeless moon dust . . . not even our day-dreams.

Man's insatiable need to conquer, his need to subjugate everything for his own purpose—when this is applied to living creatures it is often very difficult to accept, I find.

The research camp in which we were staying was used for something other than the base for the elephant study being done by Ian Douglas Hamilton. It was also used as a trapping centre for baboons—animals which were then sent to a veterinary research worker in Arusha. A wire cage containing food was in a permanent position on a dry area of the river bed. Once the unsuspecting baboon was inside it could not escape.

Each day the ranger responsible for this particular task would climb down the slope from the camp to the river bed and investigate the cage. Sometimes the baboons had managed to take the food without entering the cage. At other times they were not so fortunate. The incident which occurred while we were staying at the camp was another particularly unpleasant addition to the long list of man's uncharitableness to his fellow-creatures on this earth.

We arrived back at base for lunch one very hot day and saw, under a tree, a low oblong box, divided into two compartments and faced with a wire mesh. In one of the compartments was a female baboon. She was pregnant. She could neither stretch out fully nor could she stand up, but was crouched in mute despair in a corner of the box. We were all extremely upset and angry. It is bad enough that animals are used for scientific research and experiments, but how much worse it all seems when the animal in question is pregnant. We asked the ranger for this animal to be released, but he said it was not possible as the 'Bwana in Arusha knew the animal had been caught'. His duty was, of course, to his employer. When we questioned him about the inadequate size of the box, he said this was the travelling box, made small so that the animal could not be jolted about in transit. The baboon had been put straight into the box as it was being collected that evening. It was not, in fact, picked up until forty-eight hours later. In my horror that such a situation could exist, I wrote to John Owen and told him the whole story. His reply indicated his concern was equal to mine and he told me he would look into the matter straight away. If one could only believe this was an isolated case.

The week quickly passed and we had spent as much time in Manyara as we could spare—we now had to return to Nairobi and with little delay travel the 200 miles south-east to Tsavo, where we were to meet up again with our little elephant.

It would be difficult to imagine a more uncomfortable drive than ours from Nairobi to Lake Manyara. But our return journey was just that. We left camp at 7.30 a.m. and the first thirty-five miles took us over the same dusty roads, relieved only by the occasional glimpse of slender Masai in their red ochre robes, walking their cattle to drink or lying in unselfconsciously graceful groups under a tree. On reaching the Kenya border, where we snatched a quick lunch, Mr Mopagee's starter packed up and we were pushed rather unceremoniously on to the road to continue our journey. The rest of the trip can only be described as a nightmare, every bone in our bodies seemed to be shattered as Mr Mopagee crashed over bumps and down into holes. The handle on my door refused to close properly and I had to secure it with the strap of Bill's camera case. We arrived in Nairobi two dust-caked groaning figures, with aching heads and smarting eyes—never had bath and bed seemed so inviting!

CHAPTER TEN

The Sheldricks and an Elephant called Slowly

♣

NEW and thrilling experiences and sensations crowded in upon us. Each day held unimagined wonders. While some of our party travelled to Voi, in Tsavo, by road with the equipment, the rest of us flew in a super skywagon of the Boskovitch airline. A one-engined plane. Having survived the ordeal of Mr Mopagee-type travel I felt even planes with only one engine were preferable to yellow and black striped Land-Rovers with four wheels. We soared like a bird through the billowing dunes of white cloud which hung over Nairobi that early morning and flew effortlessly through a blue, clear sky above Nairobi Game Reserve, farm land, villages and mountains until the red Tsavo earth called out its warm welcome and we landed again on the airstrip between the thorn trees.

Simon and Laila, Bill and myself were to camp inside the park—Simon and Laila under canvas next to one of the little white bandas we had seen on our first visit. The rest of our party were staying just outside the park at the Park Inn. The banda was very simple, earth floor, makuti roof and windows covered with wire mesh—no glass. It consisted of one room where we slept and an outside porch where we installed our cooking apparatus and

A small tense grey
shape . . .

The kindness of
David Sheldrick

Pole Pole's introduction to her new friends Eleanor and Kadenge

The failure of the first 'wallow'

Enjoying a rub on a termite hill

The rhinos wanted nothing from us and James Hill but 'sugar daddies'

chairs and table. Our bedroom, which was cooler, was where we stored the tins of film and various items of camera equipment. Two beds, a table and nails on which to hang our clothes completed the room's furnishings. A cold tap behind the banda supplied us with water for cooking, washing-up and washing clothes (which we hung on hangers to 'drip dry' on the trees), and a low building beyond Mavis and Philip Hucks's house provided us with a shower where we could rid ourselves each evening of the inevitable layer of Tsavo earth. A fascinating variety of wild creatures visited us in our camp—hornbills, superb starlings, a ground squirrel, buffalo, weavers, lizards, and one early morning two wild dogs appeared behind the tent! Our eyes met for a few amazed seconds and then they turned tail and fled back into the undergrowth.

Our elephant had meanwhile arrived from Nairobi and was already a little quieter. David Sheldrick spent most of that first day with her, outside her compound, and as soon as we arrived we joined him. That afternoon he went in with her. At first she was very disquieted, making short rushes at him and trying to wedge him between her body and the posts of the compound. Firmly but gently, David let her know she had nothing to fear from him, but that any attempts to squash him or press him against the sides of the pen would be unhesitatingly discouraged. In an amazingly short time she had calmed down and was taking sweet potato tops and quartered oranges from our hands and letting us stroke her.

She was such a pretty elephant with sweeping terra-cotta eyelashes and soft spongy feet—all the names that were suggested for her seemed inappropriate for one so adorable and feminine. It was while we were watching David in the compound, coping with the animal's still unpredictable behaviour, that we became aware of a word being used constantly as he pacified her and spoke to her with kind reassurance. 'Pole, Pole . . . Pole, Pole.' 'Slowly, Slowly . . . Slowly, Slowly.' (Pole to rhyme with roly.)

'Do you think that would be a good name for her?' we asked David. 'Yes,' he replied, 'I think it would.' So Pole Pole she became.

Food tastes so good in the open. We ate our evening meal by the light of a lamp, bombarded by the Christmas beetles, praying mantis and moths which poured out of the darkness attracted to the friendly pool of light, savouring the moments of quiet stillness at the end of the day. Simon and Laila were people we felt very in tune with—silence never became a void to be filled.

I lay in bed in the darkness listening to the night sounds—the sweet shrill piping of crickets, the trumpeting of an elephant, the roar of a lion, bushes rustling and branches snapping. So close to the earth I felt a security impossible to find in our cities. The security of being part of a whole—belonging to the society of nature, not alone in the concrete isolation of modern civilization.

The first two days' work were divided between filming inside the Hucks's bus and outside their house, and spending as much time as possible with Pole Pole. One or two of the Game Rangers went in the compound with her and had a fairly lively time, but by the end of the two days she was a very different little animal from the aggressive and nervous creature we had first met. Her passion for sweet potato tops was inexhaustible and our supply soon ran out. Colin Jobson was then despatched on one of his improbable errands, fifteen miles over a very rough road, up a mountainside, to buy a lorry-load of this precious commodity from a group of astonished African villagers. Sweet potato tops were normally things to be thrown away, and the fact that here was a strange European who actually wished to pay money for them was obviously a unique experience for them! Colin, however, returned triumphantly, the lorry bulging with succulent greens.

On the third day Pole Pole was let out of her compound for the first time. Only David, Bill and the rangers were allowed to walk around with her, and the rest of us sat in cars or Land-Rovers and watched. David had warned us that one of two things would occur—she would remain with them, following them about and eating the supply of oranges and bananas they had gathered together, or she would disappear into the bush like a streak of lightning and it might be an almost impossible task to get her back. It was a risk we had to take. We need not have worried. She ambled slowly around, browsing contentedly on the trees and bushes and consuming quantities of sweet potato tops which had been left lying about in conspicuous positions. Bill and David walked beside her, occasionally stroking her, and I was very thrilled when she came over to me and took an orange which I offered to her out of the window of the Land-Rover. She followed the two men without a murmur back into her compound when time was up—completely trusting and unafraid. David then told me I could go in the compound as well, and I climbed over the barricade, my heart beating, longing for the moment when I could stand next to our little elephant and put my arms around her. She examined us all over carefully with her trunk, snuffling our shoes and sending up little red clouds of dust. It was the beginning of a short but intense friendship.

Our work for the day was not finished and we then drove nineteen miles to an isolated road—inches deep in lava dust, fine as Fuller's Earth, and here we spent nearly two hours filming a scene driving in Mr Mopagee, the choking white powdery clouds settling in our eyes and ears and hair. As we travelled, white-haired and dry-mouthed, slowly back to camp, we found ourselves in the path of an enormous herd of elephant, silhouetted in the evening light against smoke-blue clouds tinged with gold, making their massive red expedition to the river for water. We drew quickly forward to a position beyond their moving column and then turned to watch them as they deliberately made their way through the bush, one giant bull moving a little apart from the rest, his long white tusks sweeping the ground and an occasional clear trumpeting echoing in the large sky.

At supper that evening a locust alighted on my finger. I spilled my cup of coffee all over the table. I really must have some positive thoughts for good about insects!

The first day's filming with Pole Pole went without a hitch. She might have been doing it all her life! We let her out of the compound and she followed us down to the Hucks's house, where she made straight for the flower-bed and consumed a number of their prize plants —they were extremely nice about it (little did any of us

Pole Pole's 'wallow'

know what was to come). We filmed some walking shots and eating shots and after about an hour took her back to her compound. No trouble at all.

Not only was this our first day's filming with Pole Pole but also with Rufus and Ruedi, the rhinos. We drove to the pre-arranged rendezvous and waited while David got the rhinos into position about five hundred yards away behind some shrubs. On a signal he dashed towards us and Rufus dutifully steamed along behind him, followed, more slowly, by Ruedi. Too slowly, unfortunately, for the shot. It was all slightly incredible to see these two vast primeval shapes plumping through the bush towards us —on cue! Even watching it I could scarcely believe it.

I now discovered the reason behind a rather odd purchase I had been asked to make before leaving Nairobi. I had gone into Woolworths and asked a very sceptical assistant for six pounds of Sugar Daddies. This kind of Sugar Daddy is a sort of toffee lollipop on a stick. I was obviously either throwing a children's party or had a very sweet tooth. If only I could have told the assistant I was giving them to some rhinoceros friends of mine.

The Sugar Daddies were now discreetly brought from the Land-Rover and, even more carefully, a few were taken out of the box and unwrapped. (If the rhinos had seen the whole supply I dread to think what would have happened!) We gave the lollipops to David and he, in turn, held them out to Rufus and Ruedi. Oh, the squeaks of joy which filled our ears; Rufus and Ruedi were in a transport of delight, and enticed by these irresistible rewards were soon back in position. Unfortunately it had become rather hot, and after one more try and several Sugar Daddies later, we decided not to continue with the scene that day. In any case, Stub the baby rhino and the three buffalo then appeared and things got slightly out of hand—in the nicest possible way.

We had watched the habits of elephants in the wild—their feeding, their drinking and, of course, their wallowing. To care properly for Pole Pole we had to make her a wallow all of her own. Piles of red earth were put into the back of Mr Mopagee, and Bill spent a long and very hot time shovelling it all into a dip in the ground. We then turned on an outside tap and let the water seep through the ground towards our earth mound. Gradually it became nice and sticky and seemed to us of a similar consistency to those we had seen in Manyara. We walked down with Pole Pole to the wallow, anticipating the delight she was soon to experience. To our dismay she sniffed tentatively at the damp mud for a few moments and then, with a most disconsolate air, turned away and began to browse on a nearby bush. What could be wrong? Long discussions ensued and the suggestion was made by David that it could be the wrong earth. Next morning he got his rangers on the job, and a hole was dug. Very fine red earth containing no stones at all was put into it and properly dampened. Then we brought Pole Pole down. Immediately she plunged into the wallow, rolling on her side, rubbing her head, splashing the mud over her back, rolling her eyes heavenwards in ecstasy—even standing on her head! The best beauty salons never had a mud pack like this! It certainly did look very tempting and I think our delight at the elephant's unrestrained enjoyment equalled her own. That day was quite an important one in Pole Pole's life. When she had finished her wallow and had lain on the side of a termite hill, rubbing herself and spraying her damp body with dry earth, then it was time to introduce her to the other elephants, Eleanor and Kadenge. Frankly, I felt a little nervous. Pole Pole suddenly seemed so small and the other two so large and strong. What if they didn't accept her? We all moved to the Hucks's verandah and the camera was set up nearby. Pole Pole was wandering unconcernedly in the garden, and at a given moment the other elephants were brought out of the bush in front of the house. I hardly dared breathe. Trumpeting with excitement, Eleanor went quickly up to Pole Pole, who rather naturally seemed a little nervous and ran away from this strange big creature. Eleanor paced after her and at first we were not sure of the outcome of their agitated game of follow-my-leader. Gradually both the animals quietened down and Pole allowed herself to be examined all over by Eleanor's big gentle trunk. Eleanor, in fact, was overjoyed. Now, at last, she could indulge all her motherly instincts and she hardly ever, from this time, let Pole out of her sight. Pole, for her part, now had a recognizable mother figure. Kadenge tolerated Pole Pole —after all, being a male he couldn't be expected to have any motherly instincts.

Eventually all three animals were in the wallow, rolling, sliding and falling over each other in slippery joy. Bathing over, they crowded round the verandah, knocking over plant pots, eating the best dahlias and generally causing a great deal of chaos. When lunch-time came we led Pole back into her compound, but Eleanor refused to be parted from her new friend and instead of going off into the bush to browse she and Kadenge hung around the compound, Eleanor stripping bark off the compound posts in an effort to free the little one. That night it was obvious that Eleanor would not return to their sleeping quarters near the Sheldricks' house without Pole Pole, so all three elephants were led up to the pens and Pole was installed in the one normally occupied by Ruedi. Poor Ruedi got a very nasty shock when he found himself without his usual home and took rather a dim view of being put in a different pen for the night.

It was strange without Pole Pole in our camp. I missed her very much, but knew that probably she was very much happier being with her own kind and free to graze with them in the bush during the day. Whenever we did see her, during work or in the evening when we went to say goodnight to them all, she always greeted us with warmth and affection—her attitude towards us never changed. Sometimes, indeed, she would come back to us rather than follow her new friends.

Six days before we were due to leave Tsavo we had a message from Nairobi that President Kenyatta wished to see Bill's film *The Lions are Free* that same evening and wished us to be present. It was strange because it was the anniversary of his imprisonment by the British. The film show was to be held at his country home—half-an-hour's fast drive from Nairobi. At 4.15 p.m. we threw off our earth-stained shorts and shirts, had a quick shower and put on clean clothes. A light plane was waiting to fly us to Nairobi, where we were met by Monty Ruben,

George Adamson's
camp

Mtu M'Erimba, the
cook

Captivity

. . . or Freedom

. . . and Trust

driven to his house and there we made ourselves look slightly more presentable. Then, together with Hilary Ruben, we drove at a speed faster than sound to the President's home. Guards stood at the gate, flags lined the drive—and we finally ended our journey in the Social Hall, which stood near the main house and which was now filled with the President's family, ministers and servants. Also present were the German Ambassador and his wife—a German film team had made a film about Kenyatta, *Portrait of a Statesman*, and this was to be shown before our film. The President and his very lovely wife entered the hall with their children and we were introduced to him for the second time. (We had met him before in 1964 when we had been invited by Malcolm MacDonald—then the British High Commissioner—to a luncheon at State House.) He is a man of great presence and dignity.

As we watched the first film we became rather concerned that the President was not going to hear our commentary very clearly—we sometimes spoke rather quietly and the acoustics in the hall were not ideal. It was suggested to Bill that he should go to Kenyatta during the interval and give him a brief synopsis of the story. It was a good suggestion—even we, ourselves, who knew the script, could not always understand what we were saying.

The evening ended, the film was well received, and Bill presented a copy of it to the President as a gift. He accepted it and then said to us that if there was anything he could do to help, we should let him know.

We were silent. The one thing we wanted more than

anything else was something we could not ask for. The freedom of Pole Pole. We knew she was destined for the London Zoo, she was an already accepted gift, and we had been extremely fortunate in being allowed to use her for our film. Her departure had been delayed expressly for us. We did not feel entitled to ask another favour. There was another reason too. If we had managed to save our elephant from captivity and she had been allowed to remain with the others in Tsavo, eventually free to return to the wild if she so wished, then another young one would have to be captured and countless others hurt or left by the wayside as the herds were run down by the trapper. But it is very hard to be objective when one is involved. The thought of Pole Pole being put back into her crate, driven to Nairobi, flown to England to live the rest of her life in a grey world of concrete safety—never again to roll in ecstasy in a muddy wallow, to browse with Eleanor and Kadenge under the purple beauty of the Tsavo hills—these thoughts still bring pain. These unspoken thoughts were shared by us all.

Apart from one incident, the remaining busy days of filming passed smoothly. It was Simon who was the victim on this occasion. We had spent a very good morning with the three elephants, around the Hucks's house and the Land-Rover, when Kadenge suddenly became rather fed up with the whole procedure and crashed into Simon's back while he was looking through the camera lens. Simon's eyelid was cut and his back numbed. The camera fell on the ground and the lens was bent. Simon refused to complain about his own injuries, although his eye looked very swollen, and went off to do a repair job on the lens—which he managed to straighten with the aid of a hammer! Luckily, neither Simon nor the camera suffered any lasting ill-effects from the experience.

We repeated our scene with the rhinos, this time very successfully—they had just been wallowing and their skins were a deep, warm red. We spent quite a long time with them, feeding them on Sugar Daddies, stroking their soft prehensile upper lip as they closed their eyes in blissful satisfaction and swallowed the lollipops, stick and all. Our last memory of the rhinos was in front of the house, where they, aided by Stub and the buffalo, completed the final devastation of the flower-beds, watched with unflinching fortitude by the Hucks, who kindly accepted the replacement flowers we sent them.

We filmed our three elephants swimming in the river— their bodies completely submerged and their trunks waving like periscopes above the brown swirling surface. We watched them from the far bank and when, reluctantly, they left the water and splashed up towards us we stepped rather smartly behind a bush as Kadenge seemed again to be in a cheeky mood after his cooling bath! We all walked slowly back to camp, joined halfway by the six young ostriches. It seemed the most natural thing in the world.

Saying goodbye becomes increasingly difficult as one cares more. People in Africa have big personalities. Perhaps they need them in order not to be overwhelmed by the vastness of the country. They are very individual people and they make a big impact on one. I do not mean they are loud and noisy people, often the reverse, but they have a depth of thought and sense of purpose that one does not often find in our overcrowded communities. Perhaps they have fewer distractions and more time to develop these qualities.

In leaving the Sheldricks we were leaving people whose way of life and understanding were to make a lasting impression upon us. The Sheldricks and the Adamsons.

Weaver-birds nests

CHAPTER ELEVEN

The World of George Adamson

♣

WE were not leaving Kenya as we flew off from Tsavo for the last time in our light plane, we were going up to the Meru National Park to spend three days with George Adamson in his camp. And, if they were around, to do some filming with the lions. Joy's camp, where she was working on the rehabilitation of cheetah, was several miles away. Cheetah and lion do not comfortably mix!

I had never quite believed that I should one day have the good fortune to visit George's camp. From the window of the plane I could see the tiny cluster of huts nestling in the Meru wilderness. My home has always been the most important place on earth to me but, in a way, this was the other centre of my world. The plane landed in an enveloping cloud of dust on the airstrip, and as far as the eye could see stretched countless miles of thorn tree and bush, shimmering in the heat. The plane took off and we stood in the vast silence, small, insignificant specks of life. A few moments later we saw a line of dust in the distance gradually approaching. A Land-Rover pulled up a few yards away from us and out stepped George and John Baxendale, his assistant. It was a very happy meeting. We drove back down the track, carefully avoiding the numerous cracks and holes in the baked earth, and five minutes later we saw ahead of us the wire fence surrounding the camp—heightened and strengthened since Bill's last visit. George's cook, Mtu M'Erimba, held the compound gate open for us and we drove inside and turned off the engine. The camp consisted of three or four wooden huts and a tent—the kitchen hut and the living-room hut being partly opensided. John had very kindly turned out of his sleeping quarters for Bill and me and was joining the men in the 'dormitory' tent. The living-room hut was where George ate and read and talked. In it he kept his books, his provisions, his little line of White Label whisky-horses (one carved every week!) and his refrigerator. This last might seem a luxury in such remote and unsophisticated circumstances, but all ideas of self-indulgence were quickly dispelled when one opened it and one saw that its entire contents consisted of spare meat for the lions and an odd pound of butter. George did not spoil himself! We had brought a good supply of food up with us, five extra mouths to feed for three days was too much of an imposition on anyone's hospitality—and there was no nearby shop to go to if one ran out of sugar! Mtu M'Erimba was a marvellous cook. He squatted over his little fire on the floor of the cook house, frying-pan and saucepan delicately balanced on three bricks, and produced succulent breakfasts of eggs and bacon and toast and two-course dinners of soup, followed by meat and vegetables. Here, too, the water was boiled that had been brought from the river one and a half miles away. I never ceased to admire him.

The white bleached skull of a buffalo, one of the first to be killed by the lions, hung on a tree in the centre of the compound; below it on the ground was the water pan for the weaver-birds whose tree home dominated the whole camp. Discarded, imperfect nests lay scattered on the ground, and in the mornings and evenings the air was filled with the weavers' chatter as they constructed their houses and carried on endless arguments.

Fascinated as I was by the interior of the camp, it was the creatures outside its confines with whom I was most concerned. The lions. On our arrival we had seen Ugas, looking fit and well, jealously guarding the remains of a zebra under a tree just near the wire fence. Until he had moved away from his treasure it was unwise to approach him as he was behaving in a very protective manner. A little further away, lying peacefully under a bush, was Girl, my old friend, watched attentively by her own two cubs, Maya and Juno, now seventeen months old and completely wild. George, Bill and I walked over to Girl, followed by Simon with his camera, and she let me kneel down beside her and stroke her under the chin as I had done four years before. For several moments I could not speak. This same lioness was now a completely independent and successful huntress and her two cubs were the result of mating with a wild lion. Her rehabilitation was total. Later she joined us inside the compound for tea.

George's camp epitomized for me the ideal co-existence of human and animal. The animals were wild but were free to share with humans those moments when they needed their companionship. It was an arrangement of mutual satisfaction.

The sun began to sink and we all went off to the river to wash, carrying our little bundles of soap, towel and clean shirt. Simon saw a crocodile in the top pool, which caused great excitement, so we all went further down the river to smaller pools which, we hoped, the crocodile could not enter! We sat on a stone and washed the dry dust from our legs and feet, letting the cold clear water soothe our warm skin.

It was almost dark, and the forest on the edge of the river was still, peaceful, undisturbed as yet by any prowling predator. Refreshed, we returned to George's camp to eat and talk and sit under the stars, happy in the thought that only a few feet away slept, equally happy, our other four-footed friends.

Is there any sound quite as exhilarating as the voice of a lion roaring in the night? I do not think any other sound evokes such a feeling of excitement, such a sense of power. Our first night in camp the lions roared several times, beyond the wire but only a few yards from where we were lying. I turned over in bed and gazed through the open doorway into the night beyond, discerning vague shapes moving about in the grass. Was it Boy returning or the younger lions? This time it was neither, but the second night both Boy and Susua, the younger male, came into camp at about 5 a.m. We heard George talking to them by the wire, and hastening out of bed we saw, in the light of George's torch, a huge, beautiful lion, magnificently maned, weighing about 400 lbs, ac-

Reunion with George and Ugas

companied by another male, less mature but equally fine. This, then, was our old friend Boy, Girl's brother, this proud and wonderful wild animal. Here he was returning to see George after several weeks of complete independence and freedom. He had been living wild for about a year, but his visits to George had never ceased.

We were able to do some filming with Boy and Ugas, both of whom behaved like perfect gentlemen. Even when Bill, not realizing he had a small wound on top of his head, stroked Boy between his ears, the lion only turned with a low warning growl. That is one characteristic I have frequently noted about lions. They are very fair, they always give you a warning—unlike humans who, as often as not, will dispense with such courtesies.

The night before we left, the skies opened and the rain fell in solid shining sheets, transforming the earth into inches of soft treacherous mud. Our eyes were alert for scorpions, but I found only one—hiding under a jar of Marmite! The rain beat relentlessly on the roofs of the huts, here and there discovering a chink in the palm fronds and oozing its triumphant way into the hut's interior. We wondered if we were going to be able to take off in the light plane the following morning—and although when we woke we were greeted by clear, fresh skies, our doubts were not dispelled until Peter Jenkins, the Chief Game Warden of Meru (whom we had met with his family the previous day) flew over us in his high-winged little two-seater plane and dropped us a message to say the airstrip was all right.

So it was another goodbye. The wilds of Meru are a

long way from the Surrey hills—life is uncertain. When we leave those we love we can never be sure there will be a next meeting. Leaving George and the lions—well, I was leaving the other centre of my world.

CHAPTER TWELVE

A Time of Birth

♣

SPRING this year in England was especially beautiful to me. I had been ill and saw nature's forms and colours with new awareness. The apple trees' network of branches disappeared under the snowy, fragrant mass of bee-humming blossom, the nests under the eaves of the house had never sheltered so many demanding mouths, and the dogs and Macduff bounded more enthusiastically than ever over the fresh sweet young grass of the field.

It was Jonnie who brought the next animal into our lives. Jonnie, with his overpowering strength and gentle mouth. Late one afternoon in May our daughter Louise appeared at the kitchen door with the smallest deer I have ever seen dangling in her arms. 'Jonnie picked it up in his mouth,' she said, 'it was lying under a bush, but he let me take it away from him.' There wasn't a moment to be lost—the little one must be replaced under the bush in the hope that the mother would return to claim it. This was done. Three hours later it was still there, lying limply on its side. It was getting dark. We knew that if we left the deer any longer we would be risking its life. If the mother did not return for it, it was extremely improbable that, unfed, it would last the night. We brought it into the kitchen and I sat on a chair holding its uncertain life in my cupped hands.

We had a strange feeling that the deer was premature, possibly the weakling of the family—roe deer are almost always born in pairs—as its tiny hooves were soft as jelly and the base of the spine stuck sharply up under the skin. I felt anything but optimistic about its chances of survival, and obviously no time could be lost in giving it some nourishment. By an unfortunate coincidence, I had just given away my last baby's bottles and teats—Daniel was two years and no longer needed these reminders of infancy—but recalling our previous experience in Scotland, we were lucky enough to locate a teat used for rearing lambs. To our dismay this deer could not manage to get the teat in its mouth—it was far too big. The only possible solution at this point was to use an eye dropper. We found a spare one in the medicine cupboard and, having sterilized it and prepared a very weak solution of boiled water and Carnation milk and glucose, began to drop food into the pathetically small body of our second little Bambi. (We did think of other names—Bill suggested Napoleon Bonaparte—but none of them really suited him.) Again we found a tea chest, lined it with straw and buried a hot water bottle in its depths, and then began a week of constant feeding (we had now obtained antibiotic pills from the veterinary which we broke and crushed into the milk mixture) and tender care. Jonnie repeated his old role and looked after Bambi's toiletry needs with expert devotion—I could not have had a more efficient assistant. At the end of the second day Bambi could stand, and at the end of the first week I took him outside into the garden—to let him feel the warmth of the sun on his body and the grass beneath his feet. Every day he grew stronger, and so did his need for movement. His gangling legs would stride bravely over the lawn after Jonnie, only to bend and buckle as the effort proved too great.

It so happened that the children had been given two rabbits, Cottontail and Black Bob. We did not really like the idea of keeping anything in captivity, but it had been rather a question of life or death on this occasion, and so we had these two very fine young rabbits in a pen near the house. We decided to let Bambi, if it was warm, spend the day outside with them and to bring him indoors at night. We gently put Bambi near the front of the straw-lined box which stood in the centre of the pen; he stood quivering slightly on his still uncertain legs and then stepped delicately to the back of the box where the rabbits lay sleeping. Black Bob and Cottontail opened their eyes as this small stranger advanced towards them and then, with no more ado, allowed him to lie down between them, protecting and warming him with their soft furry bodies.

Flowers and trees developed into their summer fullness as the buds and insubstantial leaves of spring matured and ripened. The nests were emptied of their noisy progeny and the timid, slender body of our young Bambi strengthened and grew. The bright, clear spots that mark the fawn faded, and the soft little hooves became polished, hard and nut-brown. We made a larger pen for Bambi and the rabbits in the field enclosing brambles and shrubs and juicy clovered grasses on which he could feed at will. The six bottle feeds a day—consisting now of cow's milk—dwindled to two, to one. In a way I suppose I was loth to relinquish completely these moments of contact and the last outward signs of dependence. There had developed between us a real trust and friendship but, in fact, the end of the bottle ritual in no way meant the end of the need we felt for each other. We enjoyed being together so much. It was another arrangement of mutual satisfaction.

Every afternoon I would let Bambi out of his pen and we used to sit in the field—or rather I used to sit and he used to graze nearby, running after me if I got up and moved to another sunnier spot. The tall feathery grasses waved silkily, and the dandelions and clover revealed the secrets of their beauty as I bent closer to their green-veiled world. Jonnie and Nell were usually with us, and Boy occasionally came too, although he never accepted Bambi completely and I always had to be watchful if he came too near him. I became very impressed with Bambi's obedience, there were never any problems in getting him back in his pen, and one day I decided to break new ground and to take him for a walk through the woods. Perhaps there were certain leaves or mosses that he would require in his diet which until now I had not supplied, and this would give me a chance to observe his needs.

Our unusual little party set off slowly down the leaf-canopied path that leads through the woods. Jonnie, Nell, Bambi and myself—on later walks we were usually joined by one or more of the children, who became most concerned if Bambi strayed too far into the ferns. 'Come

Bambi II with
Jonnie, Ginny

. . . and Justin

on, Bambi, come on,' they would call, hitting their thighs with vehement hands. 'Don't worry, he'll come,' I told them. 'This is a new place for him, so much to explore, so many new smells—I wonder if he senses the other deer.' There is a small herd of deer living in our woods—they move on from time to time as roe deer will, but there always seems to be a nucleus of these small, strong, graceful animals. They often come out into the field to graze in the early morning and the evening, and we all crowd to the windows to look at them. I often wonder if they know they are safe there—I hope they do.

On our first walk Bambi stayed quite close to me on the path, the tall rustling trees, the shrubs, the carpet of ferns—this was the world he came from, but he had left it too soon for our walk to awaken any memories. A snapping stick, or a dog suddenly running through the undergrowth, caused him to stop in his tracks, one front foot slightly lifted in the air, ears pointed forward, shiny nose trembling. It was all bewildering and I soon turned and retraced our steps. Bambi's sigh of relief as we entered the familiar territory of the garden was almost visible!

From then on we went for a woodland walk almost every day, Bambi's courage and curiosity growing by leaps and bounds until one afternoon, halfway along the path, he suddenly sprang forward, jumping over ferns and fallen branches and within seconds had disappeared from view. I stood quite still, hardly daring to breathe, realizing with a shock that this was a risk I had been taking from the moment these walks began. The desire for freedom—it must be stronger than anything. And of course I understood this, but my fear was that Bambi was still too young to face the hazards of the wild. Not only was he alone, with no mother to guide and teach him, but through his association with us he had no fear of human beings. And the fear of human beings is a wild animal's greatest protection. What a comment on our species. How can we possibly live with this on our consciences? But we can. The need to dominate, to impose, is too great—otherwise we would not have animals in zoos or in circuses. We could no more stare and chatter and grin at a lion sitting in dull lethargy on a cold stone floor, or a monkey doomed to a barred and treeless isolation, than we could go and laugh at the prisoners in Wandsworth or Brixton. The only difference being that the lion and the monkey have done no wrong and the prisoners have, as judged by their fellow human beings, committed some crime. 'This even-handed Justice.'

The seconds stretched in my mind into minutes and my eyes strained into the depths of the wood, wanting more than anything to see a flash of brown between the trees. Suddenly I heard a light but forceful sound coming towards me, and I saw Bambi leaping with undiminished joy and vigour. He stopped beside me on the path, for a few panting moments, and then he took flight again and disappeared into the distance on the other side of the track. For some reason I no longer was afraid. He had come back and I knew he would again.

This became the pattern of our walks. Each time we penetrated further into the trees, joining the stream at the lower end of the woods and returning up the whole length of the field. I would gather clover and favourite leaves and plants and amble heavily laden up the sloping meadow, Bambi nibbling the sweet juicy flowers as they trailed from my arms. September cooled into October and it was obvious that we must come to some decision about the deer's future. He was growing big. His loose baby hair had gone, his coat was thick and sleek and brown and the little buttons were forming on top of his head, where next year his horns would be. It was not a question at this point of choice between captivity and freedom, but of which captivity was preferable. We knew that if we kept Bambi we would possibly be storing up future problems—we had been told that hand-reared males can be very threatening at certain times of the year, when they have rubbed the velvet off their horns, and they become impossible to approach.

Philip Wayre, who created the Norfolk Wild Life Park, says, 'In my experience hand-reared males become extremely aggressive when adult, particularly towards human beings and to other deer kept in the same paddock.' We realized that our situation needed careful deliberation. Not only ourselves, but our children would have to understand that during certain months going into Bambi's enclosure was out of the question. We decided to work in stages.

The following weekend we started building a new, extremely large enclosure, encompassing part of the woods, the stream and the field. It was surrounded by a four-foot fence of wire netting, and inside was a covered, strawlined shelter. This enclosure was to be the future home of Bambi, Black Bob and Cottontail (whom we had decided to let run free). The enclosure was completed in early November and the three friends moved into their new home.

It is possible, and even probable, that next spring, when the snows have disappeared from the hills, we may take Bambi to a remote, unpeopled area of Scotland and set him free. Now he is still too young, but when he matures and his desire for freedom is frustrated, making him excitable and dangerous, there would be no justification in denying him the chance to return to his natural habitat. Roe deer are able to return to a wild state in a remarkably short space of time, and as much as I know I would miss him, I would rather he was free to live for the purpose for which he was born.

CHAPTER THIRTEEN

A Time of Discovery

♣

THERE can be no real conclusion to this book. No tidy ending. As long as I and the surviving animals about whom I have written continue to live, the story can have no end.

As I look out into the garden and see our own animals and look past the garden to the woods and sense the other animal life that is sheltered there, I gaze beyond all this into the future with its uncertainties for all life. We can, to a limited extent, plan the future of those within our care, while they are in our care—our dogs, our cats, our birds and all those animals we cherish so deeply and upon whom so many people depend for giving affection and for receiving it. But our love and concern for animals should go beyond those within our personal environment, as the care and concern for humans should also. We should, I believe, see the world as a whole, see nature in its entirety and realize the importance of humans being part of the animal world and animals being part of theirs. It is only in this way that we can prevent the complete destruction of our environment and perhaps, ultimately, of ourselves.

We are moulding and shaping our future with little

concern for anything but ourselves. We are eliminating animals from our earth. But when the last animal has vanished, what will there be left to look at—each other. To dominate—each other. To destroy—each other.

I cling to the beauty and strength of nature and all wild creatures with a passion born of certainty that only through them can I retain my perspective about life and my own part in it. I know too that as man impatiently smears the surface of the earth with his concreting fingers, the days of the badger, the leopard and the hartebeest are numbered.

We must begin to think about animals in a different way, for only then will we be able to speak about them differently. Do we really understand what we are saying when we use phrases like 'he lives just like an animal' or 'he is no better than an animal'? On what do we base our derogatory attitude? Is it simply that we know so little about the other inhabitants of the world from whom we can learn so much, about them and, perhaps, ourselves?

Could we not learn something to our advantage from the social behaviour and loyalty of the elephant, the devoted parenthood of the coucal, the courage and dedication to family life of the warthog? Must we continue to be the only species unable to co-exist with the rest of the world's creatures? Wildebeest, zebra and warthog, elephant, impala and baboon manage to live in harmony. Most predators rarely kill except for food. Must we be the only enemy to all life?

Because of human deceit we have come to mistrust our fellow-humans, and we carry this mistrust into our attitude towards animals.

George Adamson knows the importance of trust. Without it, could he have held the basin of water for Boy who at the time the photograph was taken had been independent for two years and who had recently been severely injured in an encounter with a buffalo? Could he have held Boy's head in his arms while the anaesthetizing injection he had given him took effect, so that the lion might have his badly broken leg pinned and stitched by the Harthoorns—the two brilliant veterinaries who flew from Nairobi to perform this unique operation in the bush? George has left Meru now and gone to the Adamsons' home in Naivasha with Boy, to stay with him until he is fit to return again, if possible, to a natural life.

We know so little, we understand even less. What do we think, for example, about the warthog—except that he is ugly? But is he ugly? By whose standards? We are quick to reject and condemn and slow to learn, to investigate. We presume to judge and is this not a conceit? Should we not try to understand and respect the warthog for what he is—another member of the animal world to which we also belong? Bill thinks that we should try. He is now making a film in Kenya about these individual, brave little animals. He is forging another link in the chain.

It will be an opportunity to learn, a time of discovery. As all life should be.